A VERY DIFFERENT WAR

T0358150

RAAF Operations in the Korean War

Owen Zupp

RAAF
HISTORY AND HERITAGE

The publishing of this book has been funded and managed by the History and Heritage Branch, Royal Australian Air Force.

All inquiries should be made to the publishers.
Big Sky Publishing Pty Ltd
PO Box 303, Newport, NSW 2106, Australia
Phone: 1300 364 611
Email: info@bigskypublishing.com.au
Web: www.bigskypublishing.com.au

Series: Australian Air Campaign Series; 8

 A catalogue record for this
book is available from the
NATIONAL National Library of Australia
LIBRARY
OF AUSTRALIA

Cover design and typesetting by Think Productions, Melbourne

CONTENTS

RAAF Operations in the Korean War is one of ten books by Owen Zupp. His first book, *Down to Earth*, was published in 2006 by Grub Street (UK). His biography about his father, titled *Without Precedent*, has been even more widely acclaimed. An award-winning aviation writer, his work has been featured in magazines around the globe including *FlyPast* (UK), *Airliner World* (UK), *Aviation History* (US), *Plane & Pilot* (US), *Global Aviator* (South Africa) and *Australian Aviation*. Owen has won Australasian Aviation Press Club awards and is an airline captain with more than 35 years' flight experience. He is also an officer in the RAAF Reserve.

SERIES FOREWORD

The Australian Air Campaign Series produced by Air Force's History and Heritage Branch will focus on four sub-series themed book titles:

- Campaigns, Operations and Battles,
- Capability and Technology,
- Bases and Airfields, and
- People.

These themed titles are intended to explore specific facets of the Air Force from its inception in 1921. What they will reveal are unique insights, providing the reader with a greater appreciation and deeper understanding of those aspects that have shaped the Air Force's history and heritage.

Importantly, each of these publications will be sourced from official records and research, often including first-hand accounts. While these publications are endorsed for studies in military history, the range of topics will provide an ideal conduit for the broadest of audiences, to pursue and learn more about the many aspects that have contributed to the development of Australia's Air Force.

Apart from becoming a significant point of reference, these publications will ultimately acknowledge the bravery, ingenuity, resilience – in essence, the service and sacrifice which is the hallmark of those who have served and continue to serve in the Air Force.

Robert Lawson OAM
Air Commodore
Director-General History and Heritage – Air Force
August 2023

FOREWORD

Following World War Two, the Royal Australian Air Force maintained a presence in Japan as part of the British Commonwealth Occupation Forces until this role drew to a close in 1950. With their aircraft prepared for the sea voyage home, personnel enjoyed a final party on the eve of their departure for Australia. On the Korean Peninsula, the Korean People's Army gathered north of the 38th Parallel, then moved south across the border. A few hours later, a phone call to the RAAF base at Iwakuni called for the Mustangs of No 77 Squadron to be reactivated and readied for operations.

The party was over; they would not be shipping home – the Korean War had begun.

Over the next three years, the Royal Australian Air Force would serve with distinction in a broad range of operations alongside other members of the United Nations Command as the conflict moved north and south over the length of the peninsula. Their combined efforts would draw high praise, with 77 Squadron being awarded the Republic of Korea Presidential Unit Citation, and current members of the squadron are still entitled to wear the insignia.

Throughout my career, I continued to learn and better understand the significance of Australia's contribution to the 'Forgotten War'. Representing the RAAF at a reunion of the Chosin Few, I met 2,500 remaining veterans of the US 1st Marine Division who, after being encircled by Chinese forces, bravely fought a 17-day brutal battle of survival. Throughout the reunion, I was told time and time again of 77 Squadron's significant contribution to their survival. Later, as Chief of Defence Force, I was privileged to be briefed by a junior pilot from 102 Squadron, Republic of Korea Air Force about 77 Squadron's exploits and sacrifices in helping save his nation. Most moving for me though, was sitting with an Australian veteran at The War Memorial of Korea in the middle of modern day Seoul, a vibrant city that had grown out of the rubble. The veteran was in tears, remembering back to 1952, his mates, the losses – and all he could say was 'it was worth it.'

While the Korean War has been, on occasions, overshadowed by the world war that preceded it, the conflict represented a significant chapter in the evolution of today's Air Force. Beyond being the first Commonwealth air force to fly on operations during the Korean War, the RAAF both entered the jet age in 1951 and achieved its final air combat victory in 1953. The war gave rise to a number of pilots who would ultimately lead the RAAF in the future, and the lessons learnt would provide the impetus to create the fighter combat instructor course.

These achievements and advancements came at a heavy cost, with more than 40 personnel paying the supreme sacrifice. Including those pilots serving on exchange from the Royal Air

Force, it is a number that represents a loss rate of around one in four pilots who served. This book pays tribute to them, many of whom have no known grave.

It is an honour to provide the foreword to this book by Owen Zupp and through its words recognise those who served with the RAAF in the Korean War. Their significant contribution should never be forgotten.

Air Chief Marshal
Mark Binskin, AC (Retd)

AUTHOR'S NOTE

The Royal Australian Air Force's involvement in the Korean War has always been of personal interest to me. My father, then Sergeant Phillip Zupp, flew 201 missions with No 77 Squadron. His fading photographs and tattered logbook fascinated me from a young age, as did the blue nylon flying suit, curiously with a United States Air Force and winged insignia emblazoned upon the shoulder.

In researching this book, I delved into the Unit History Sheets, Tactical Reports, Pilot Narratives and numerous texts; the names on the pages were familiar. They were gentlemen from my boyhood in whose company I had silently listened and, in manhood, continued to listen to and even share a scone or a beer with on occasions.

My research also further reinforced my belief that, in writing, it is always more difficult to be concise than it is to be expansive.

The squadron's operations provided an appropriate vehicle by which to steer the chronology of the RAAF involvement in Korea, but the contribution of the RAAF was greater than that of a single unit. In this book, every armourer, mechanic, clerk, nurse, chaplain, airman and officer deserves mention by name for their efforts in a conflict that has often been overlooked. However, in the interests of conciseness, that is not possible.

As such, any oversight on my part is in no way reflective of the RAAF personnel who served so admirably through the Korean War. To all who served and to those that waited at home, this book is humbly dedicated.

Owen Zupp

June 2022

PROLOGUE

In the record of world events, the Korean War was caught between the enormity of the Second World War and the controversy of Vietnam. Although it may have slipped through the cracks of history for some, it represented a major global shift as two opposing ideologies squared off in 1950 and the Cold War heated up. The fledgling United Nations (UN) was called to act and validate its existence in a world witnessing the dawn of the nuclear age.

Australia was one of 51 founding members of the UN, of which 21 were committed to supporting South Korea. At the outbreak of the Korean War, Australia became the first country after the United States to commit units from all three of its military services. Within days of the North Koreans surging south across the 38th Parallel, the Royal Australian Air Force (RAAF) was flying missions to Korea from its base at Iwakuni in Japan.

In the ensuing three years, the RAAF came to gain respect among its peers and the attention of the opposing military powers. A relatively small aerial force overall, No 30 Communication Unit (later No 30 Transport Unit and then No 36 Squadron) and No 77 Squadron served in a range of valuable operational roles throughout the conflict, ably supported by No 491 Maintenance Squadron and No 391 (Base) Squadron.

When the war reached a crisis point, with UN forces pinned down at Pusan and under threat of being pushed off the peninsula and into the sea, the RAAF was at the epicentre. When the wounded needed to be repatriated to Japan, the RAAF Nursing Service and the C-47s crisscrossed the Sea of Japan. And when air power shifted into the jet age, the RAAF was there to not only witness the transition but to innovate.

This concise history of the RAAF's involvement in the Korean War uses the operations of No 77 Squadron as a timeline against which the course of the war can be logically tracked but casts the net wider to examine the roles of the transport unit, the nurses, the ground crews, the pilots who became prisoners of war, and those who still have no known resting place. The Korean War thrust the RAAF both into the Cold War and the fledgling concept of limited war where strategy was devised within the limitations of policy. Its transition into a jet fighting force was not without challenges and losses, although ultimately a generation of Air Force leaders emerged from the ranks of sergeant pilots and junior officers who underwent their baptism of fire on the Korean Peninsula. Many of the lessons learned in air combat over Korea created a legacy that endures today in the form of No 2 Operational Conversion Unit and the Fighter Combat Instructor course.

When North Korea invaded the South on 25 June 1950, the RAAF was already held in high regard by members of the British Commonwealth Occupation Force and the United States Air Force. Involved from the first days of the war, through to the Armistice three years later, that reputation was only enhanced. This book is a tribute to those who served and particularly to those who did not return.

Chapter 1
LAND OF THE
MORNING CALM

The Korean Peninsula highlighting United Nations airfields, 'MiG Alley' and the 38th Parallel.

The Korean people best know their land as *Chosun*, or the 'land of the morning calm'. The Korean Peninsula extends south like a pistol grip from its northern border with China, marked by the Yalu and Tumen rivers. To its east, across the Sea of Japan, lies Japan, closer than Sydney is to Canberra.

It is a land of devastatingly rugged terrain with jagged ridgelines, deep valleys and numerous peaks towering beyond 5,000 feet (1,524 metres). Through the stifling summer heat, visibility is corrupted by haze and, in the sub-zero winter, the snow masks geographic features from the air. It was not a landscape that welcomed the RAAF pilots who had ventured north from their wide, brown land.

The line that today divides the Korean Peninsula at the 38th Parallel belies the greater portion of Korean history. Predominantly rural in its existence and isolated in its global philosophy, for centuries Korea had been unified, albeit with internal feuds between ruling families. Japan twice invaded its shores in the 16th century, but it was the progressive inroads made in the late 19th century that would ultimately carry the greatest impact.

From 1876, Japan continued to escalate its influence and military presence in Korea until 1910 when the Japan–Korea Annexation Treaty was signed, formally placing Korea under Japanese rule. It was a situation that would continue until Japan's defeat in 1945 and give rise to growing resentment among the Korean population. This unrest initially stemmed from the Japanese progressively displacing Korean landowners from their farms, reducing them from owners to tenants and calling for substantial taxes to be paid. Furthermore, when Japan suffered a rice shortage in 1918, it drew upon Korean rice production to the detriment of the peasant population. While Korea's agriculture predominantly lay in the south, the north of the country was rich in mineral deposits of coal, iron and limestone.

In the late 1930s, as Japan geared up for war, it increasingly used the native population as forced labour in factories and mines, with many thousands dying. The harsh existence under Japanese rule only descended further into misery during the years of the Second World War with the infamous drafting of thousands of Korean women into brothels across Asia to serve the Japanese military as 'comfort women'. With the war in a desperate state for the Japanese, Korean men were drafted into the Japanese military from 1944.

Between the detonation of the atomic bombs over Hiroshima and Nagasaki in August 1945, the USSR declared war on Japan, with troops rapidly advancing through Manchuria, where the Japanese had defeated the Russian Army in 1905. Recognising the first strides of the communist advance could result in the entire peninsula falling under Russian rule, the United States hastily sought to stake its claim in Korea and halt the southward progression of Soviet forces. Using a National Geographic map, two United States colonels, who would both later serve as the Secretary of State, opted for a model similar to the division of Germany into occupied zones.

For this purpose, they selected the 38th Parallel north line of latitude, which divided Korea close to midway geographically. Importantly, the traditional capital of Seoul fell in the southern United States-aligned sector, along with the greater proportion of arable land. The Soviets agreed to the proposal; significantly, no Koreans were consulted on the planned division and governance of their homeland.

It was originally seen as a short-term solution. Korea would be self-governed; towards this goal, two Korean leaders emerged, each backed by their respective sponsors. In the Soviet North, Kim Il Sung had been a guerrilla fighter against the Japanese occupation. In the US-backed South, it was Syngmann Rhee who had been imprisoned for anti-Japanese activities before escaping to the United States in 1904. Both men had returned to Korea from exile and envisioned a unified Korea.

In the South in 1948, Rhee was elected as the first President of the Republic of Korea, a position he would hold until 1960. North of the parallel, Kim Il Sung became the first Premier of the Democratic People's Republic of Korea, a position he would hold until his death in 1994, albeit with a change in title to President in 1972.

To this backdrop, Kim Il Sung believed there was unrest within the South Korean Army and that the population would welcome reunification of the peninsula, even if it was under the communist North. In 1949, he sought Josef Stalin's support to invade the South but the Russian leader was hesitant. The Chinese People's Liberation Army, which could support such an act, was still involved in a civil war within its borders. However, by 1950 the situation had changed and Stalin contemplated an invasion of South Korea. He believed the United States would not become involved in a potential nuclear confrontation for the sake of the distant Korean Peninsula.

In February 1950, Stalin and Mao Zedong signed the Sino–Soviet Treaty of Friendship, Alliance and Mutual Assistance which provided China with both military and economic aid. In April, Stalin authorised Kim Il Sung to invade the South but only if he could garner the support of China and in the knowledge that Russia would not directly participate in combat. When Kim Il Sung met with Mao, the Chinese leader was desperate to retain the Russian aid provided by the treaty and agreed to support the North Korean plan.

Despite Stalin stating Russians would not be involved in combat, experienced Soviet military advisors were sent to assist North Korea with planning. Ultimately, Russian pilots would not only train Chinese and North Korean pilots but actively, and anonymously, fly combat missions and duel with United Nations pilots.

Throughout June 1950, border skirmishes took place along the 38th Parallel as Kim Il Sung positioned his troops north of the parallel in preparation for the advance southward. On 25 June 1950, approximately 100,000 North Korean People's Army (NKPA)* troops crossed the 38th Parallel and the Korean War began.

The United Nations was now confronted with its first substantial challenge since its inception in October 1945. On 27 June 1950, the United Nations Security Council declared North Korea's actions constituted a breach of the peace and adopted Resolution 83, recommending United Nations members provide military assistance to South Korea. Russia could have vetoed the resolution but was not in attendance as it was boycotting the proceedings in protest of Taiwan's nationalist government occupying China's seat on the council rather than Mao's People's Republic of China.

The next day, Seoul fell to the NKPA and, on 2 July 1950, North American P-51 Mustangs of No 77 Squadron RAAF flew their first missions of the Korean War.

* Officially the North Korean forces were known as the Korean People's Army (KPA), but NKPA was also in use and is included here to ensure distinction.

Chapter 2
POST-WAR RAAF – BCOF

In February 1946, the divisions between North and South Korea were already deepening. The chasm between Russian and American policies in their respective zones led to an increasing division of the population such that, by May, a permit was required for Koreans to pass between North and South. The beginning of 1946 also saw the Royal Australian Air Force (RAAF) begin its commitment to the British Commonwealth Occupation Force (BCOF) in Japan.

In the aftermath of the Second World War, the Allied nations sought to enforce the unconditional surrender Japan had signed in September 1945; this formed the primary task of the BCOF. It called for oversight of the repatriation of Japanese servicemen and the discovery and destruction of wartime materiel.

The BCOF drew upon military contingents from across the Commonwealth, including Great Britain, India, Canada, New Zealand and Australia. Contributions of land, sea and air forces combined under a leadership commanded by an officer of the Australian Army, in the first instance, Lieutenant General John Northcott.

The badge worn by members of the British Commonwealth Occupation Force. (Australian War Memorial)

The air force component of the BCOF was known as the British Commonwealth Air Forces of Occupation – Japan (BCAIR) and comprised units from the RAAF, Royal Air Force (RAF), Royal Indian Air Force and the Royal New Zealand Air Force (RNZAF). The RAAF's initial contribution was No 81 Fighter Wing and its three Mustang fighter squadrons – 76, 77 and 82. These units were based at Bofu (Hōfu) Airfield in the Yamaguchi Prefecture,

90 kilometres to the south-west of Hiroshima, as the initial choice of Iwakuni Airfield was near capacity with RAF and RNZAF units already in place.

The three squadrons had relocated to Bofu from Labuan, Borneo, in March 1946, where they had been based since the cessation of hostilities. In a substantial three-stage journey, the Mustangs first flew to Clark Field in the Philippines, then Naha Airfield, Okinawa, before the final long overwater stage to Japan. Sadly, three Mustangs of No 82 Squadron, in company with their Mosquito escort aircraft, were lost in inclement weather during the final stage to Bofu on 18 March.

The three fighter squadrons had been preceded by the members of No 381 (Base) Squadron which had been formed in January 1946 at Labuan under the command of Wing Commander Jack R Kinninmont DFC and Bar. Created to provide logistical and administrative support, the unit travelled by ship to Japan, arriving in Kure Bay on 21 February. Also departing in advance of the Mustangs were No 481 Maintenance Squadron and No 5 Airfield Construction Squadron (5ACS).

The first Mustang to land in Japan was that of 81 Wing's commanding officer, Wing Commander Glen Cooper DFC. From their base in Bofu, the wing undertook surveillance and patrol sorties as a component of BCAIR. Overflying the various prefectures, the Mustangs sought to locate remaining weapons and ordnance yet to be found. Patrolling the Inland Sea of Japan, the RAAF flew in support of the Royal Australian Navy to intercept smuggling operations of both goods and Korean immigrants to Japan. Spraying DDT insecticide over areas manned by the BCOF also fell to No 77 Squadron.

A Mustang serving with the BCOF over Iwakuni. (Ces Sly)

Weather provided a constant obstacle, ranging from low cloud and rain to the occurrence of typhoons. By mid-1946, 5ACS was constantly challenged with keeping the runway at Bofu serviceable; in the absence of adequate hardstands for parking and hangars for maintenance, No 481 Squadron performed admirably to keep the Mustangs operational under difficult conditions.

Training was also a pivotal undertaking for the squadrons. Lectures on armament, airmanship, oxygen systems, engine handling and formation flying were complemented by briefings on aerial gunnery and dive-bombing techniques, notably using rockets. The lessons were repeatedly put into practice in the cockpit, flying mock air-to-air and air-to-ground sorties, firepower demonstrations, Army-support exercises and simulated strikes on naval shipping.

Operating from Miho airfield in September, No 77 Squadron fired a total of 665 rockets as part of a course of air-to-ground training, achieving excellent results with an average accuracy of 14.2 metres, although it was noted the accuracy waivered in later dives as pilots experimented with their own techniques.

As 1947 drew to a close amid the bitter winds and snow of a Japanese winter, maintenance of the Mustangs became even more difficult with the ground crews and aircraft exposed to the elements. It also heralded a change in the construct of BCAIR with January 1948 seeing the RAF withdraw most of its BCOF units from Japan, including its two Spitfire squadrons from Iwakuni. It was decided the RAAF units would move to Iwakuni from March 1948, although initial operations were limited as 5ACS set about constructing a new airstrip.

In July, No 81 Wing participated in a major exercise titled Operation *Platypus*. Based out of Takamatsu airfield, the exercise simulated the wing moving onto an airfield, recently abandoned by an enemy, and commencing operations. The Mustangs were tasked with defending against inbound attacking fighters and bombers while making their own attacks upon enemy shipping and airfields.

The following month, a BCAIR Administrative Instruction echoed the scaling back of the BCOF being implemented. In September, all No 81 Wing units were to be disbanded, with 77 Squadron becoming 'RAAF Component Japan', although that title did not last long. Once again known as No 77 Squadron, the Mustangs returned to their familiar roles of patrolling, surveillance and training.

November welcomed Wing Commander Geoff Newstead as the new commanding officer of the squadron, taking over from Squadron Leader Ron Susans. By the end of 1948, the squadron had nearly 300 personnel and operated 40 Mustangs, two C-47 Dakotas, four Wirraways and two Austers. Furthermore, it was the only BCOF flying unit remaining in Japan.

The scaling back of the BCOF and BCAIR was reflective of the greater reduction in numbers of the broader RAAF. At the end of the Second World War, more than 173,000 men and

Auster A11-60

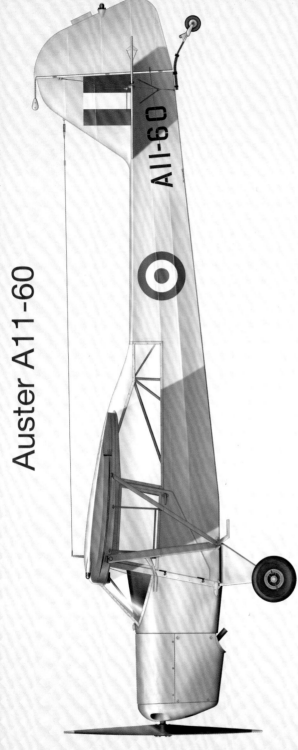

Taylorcraft Auster Mk.V (Juanita Franzi)

Auster A11-60 was one of two of the type allocated to No 91 Wing in Japan. It was written off in March 1952 after a crash at an airfield at Yamaguchi, about 70 kilometres from Iwakuni.

TECHNICAL DATA

DESCRIPTION:
Three-seat observation and communications aircraft.

POWER PLANT:
One 97-kW (130-hp) Lycoming 0-290 piston engine.

DIMENSIONS:
Span 10.97 m (36 ft 0 in); length 6.83 m (22 ft 5 in); height 2.44 m (8 ft 0 in).

WEIGHTS:
Empty 499 kg (1,100 lb); loaded 839 kg (1,850 lb).

PERFORMANCE:
Max speed 209 km/h (130 mph); cruising speed 180 km/h (112 mph); initial climb 244 m/min (800 ft/min); service ceiling 4,600 m (15,100 ft); range 402 km (250 miles) or 740 km (460 miles) with long-range tank fitted.

women were serving in the RAAF, however, that number had drastically reduced to just over 8,000 by 1948. As a consequence, No 77 Squadron was the largest unit in the RAAF at the time.

In January 1949, the Japanese people went to the polls and the squadron's Austers were tasked with dropping leaflets encouraging people to vote in the lead-up to the election, while on the ground, squadron personnel visited polling booths in the form of surveillance teams. By this time a Japanese workforce of 50 labourers was employed at Iwakuni in numerous support roles.

The families of serving members were also permitted to live on base in an area termed the Dependents Estate. Many of the families employed local Japanese and house boys to assist with basic tasks such as laundry and shopping. After being at war, the ability to fly training operations by day and return to the family at day's end resembled a normal life, albeit far from home.

The elections coincided with increased security concerns as well as the emergence of political activity relating to the Communist Party. A Korean national was being held for flying a North Korean flag and 500 members of the League of Korean Residents, or Korean League, had gathered to protest his incarceration. The squadron's intelligence reports for March 1949 relate that the group had previously distributed pamphlets denouncing the common enemy, the capitalists. In September, the Japanese Government's order to dissolve the League of Korean Residents in Japan as an 'anti-democratic and terrorist' group was the first step in a campaign to outlaw all leftist organisations known to have participated in recent communist-inspired acts of violence.

Bofu, Japan, 1947. Aircrew and ground staff of No 82 Squadron RAAF, British Commonwealth Occupation Force, in front of a Mustang. (Australian War Memorial)

Throughout 1949, the RAAF contingent continued to train and maintain its operational standards, with high-level bombing, rocketing and ground attack at the forefront. In December, 77 Squadron distinguished itself at the Far East Air Force gunnery competition held at the United States Air Force (USAF) Base at Yokota. Competing against several USAF fighter groups, including units operating F-80 Shooting Star jets, the squadron came second by only three points, lamenting an opportunity to win with valuable points lost in the skip-bombing section of the competition.

The disappointment was offset to some degree by the performance of Flight Lieutenant John 'Bay' Adams winning the highest individual points award. Adams was a flight commander, having served in the Second World War flying Hawker Tempests in Europe with No 3 Squadron RAF. He had served alongside the French ace and author Pierre Clostermann and been responsible for shooting down two V-1 flying bombs and sharing in the destruction of a third. Of Adams, Clostermann reflected, in his book *The Big Show*, that, '... he was quite imperturbable and feared neither God nor the Devil'.

The cooperation and friendly competition between the RAAF and USAF at this time was the forerunner of what would become a close relationship in the years ahead. It also offered a mutual insight into the conduct of operations and the capability of the respective squadrons from which a level of trust and respect grew.

In February 1950, Wing Commander Newstead passed command of the squadron to Wing Commander Louis Spence DFC. Spence had flown in the Middle East with No 3 Squadron RAAF and been awarded the Distinguished Flying Cross (DFC) and been mentioned in despatches for his two aerial victories and numerous ground-attack sorties.

The unrest on the Korean Peninsula was an undertone not detected by many of the squadron's staff other than being mentioned in the monthly intelligence reports that noted occasional protests among the Korean population and the rise of communist activity in Japan. However, tensions were increasing on the peninsula with small engagements taking place along the 38th Parallel.

With authorities aware of the increasing tension, in March 1950, two Australian officers were positioned in Korea as military observers to assess the situation along the border at the request of the United Nations Commission on Korea. One was an Army officer, Major Stuart Peach, and the other was Squadron Leader Ronald Rankin DFC and Bar. A schoolteacher by trade, Rankin was an Australian rugby union representative before the Second World War which saw him serve as a pilot flying Bristol Blenheims and Beaufighters.

In company with an interpreter, the two officers surveyed the situation and prepared a report outlining that the South Korean forces were in defensive positions with no ability to conduct an attack upon the North, while the North Koreans seemed to be deployed offensively. The report would come to be known as the Peach–Rankin Report and was later pivotal in discrediting claims South Korea had attacked the North.

The unit's departure was to be marked by a party across the coming weekend. The Sergeants Mess was decorated in the theme of a pirate's hideaway, complete with a plank to walk on entering and a series of rubber dinghies dispersed around the 'island'. Those not partaking of sufficient liquor were cast into the brig until they had met the required standard. The event would come to be known as 'The Shipwreck Party'.

Wing Commander Spence and his wife attended, although not dressed in the pirate garb worn by others, opting to wear their tennis outfits, claiming they were playing a game when the ship went down. The couple retired at a respectable hour to allow celebrations to continue unimpeded by the CO's presence. The party continued into the small hours of the morning and with no further flying operations planned, those present were determined to 'drink the bar dry' so as to not let the Americans have their residual bar stocks.

As dawn broke on Sunday 25 June 1950, the Korean People's Army surged south across the 38th Parallel in unison with artillery fire. The Korean War had begun.

Sergeant Ray Trebilco was the orderly sergeant that took the call from the Headquarters of the United States Fifth Air Force at 11 am on Sunday, requesting the squadron go on immediate standby as North Korea had invaded the South. Initially, Trebilco is reputed to have told the USAF duty officer to 'pull the other one' and hung up. Trebilco passed the news to the Operations Officer, Squadron Leader Graham Strout, who immediately drove to the residence of Wing Commander Spence.

Some officers, including Flight Lieutenant 'Bay' Adams, were initially sceptical but gradually the reality of the situation hit home and the pilots gathered to be briefed by Spence. The Mustangs needed to be readied, with some already coated in inhibitor for the voyage home to Australia. Drop tanks were fitted, weapons armed, and pilots placed on standby as No 77 Squadron pivoted from a state of wind-down to a war footing overnight.

The chain of events had caught Pilot 3 (Flight Sergeant) Milt Cottee totally off guard as he recalled during his recording for the Australians at War Film Archive:

'Why are we arming our aeroplanes?'

I raced out of the place and down to the tarmac to see what is going on.

'Hey, what is going on, fellows?'

'North Korea has overrun South Korea.'

Where is Korea? It was almost that, I knew it was over there somewhere, but I didn't know much about it.

'What are they doing?'

'They have run across the Parallel'.

'The Parallel, what's the Parallel?'

Mustangs lined up at Iwakuni. The aircraft nearest the camera bears the words 'Swift to Destroy' on its nose.
(Australian War Memorial)

The pilots assisted ground crews in arming the aircraft and carried out daily inspections of their Mustangs. However, Ray Trebilco would recollect they knew nothing of the North Korean People's Air Force and desperately sought information from their Intelligence Officer. They did not possess any knowledge of the types of aircraft they operated, or even their markings. The RAAF was now on the threshold of a war in which it would actively participate for three years.

THE P PILOT RANK SYSTEM

The Korean War saw close cooperation between the air forces of the United Nations with shared airfields and often shared facilities within. For the pilots of the Royal Australian Air Force (RAAF), this led to some confusion as, while the American pilots were all commissioned officers, the RAAF retained pilots within its strength that were non-commissioned officers – sergeants, flight sergeants and warrant officers. Until the implementation of the RAAF College at Point Cook, which saw pilots graduate as pilot officers, other RAAF pilots received their wings and the rank of sergeant on the successful completion of training. It was an arrangement that endured until the late 1950s.

As the Americans considered all pilots to be officers, they were duly invited to join their allies in the Officers Mess. It was an awkward situation that found various solutions that ranged from the Australian sergeants wearing the rank of pilot officer or flying officer on their flying suit or displaying no rank at all.

The wreath was worn on the sleeve in place of chevrons, with stars being added as the pilot rose through the non-commissioned officer ranks. (via Owen Zupp)

The confusion was even greater in the early stages of the Korean War when the pilots wore the rank under the 'P System'. The P System originated with the Royal Air Force (RAF) following the Second World War but had been abandoned as unworkable by 1950. Under the system, pilots wore a laurel wreath on their sleeves, rather than chevrons, or stripes. On graduation, they received a single star to place within the wreath, designating them as P4, or roughly equivalent to a corporal. After six months, they received a second star to become P3, or equivalent to a sergeant; P2, flight sergeant, and P1, warrant officer. There was a range of inconsistencies within the system. A P4 Pilot could enter the Sergeants Mess but on matters of discipline was ranked lower than a corporal. A pilot could fly an operational mission and then be assigned guard duty.

The RAAF followed the lead of the RAF and disbanded the system, with squadron operational records no longer referring to the P System from March 1951.

Chapter 3
MUSTANGS INTO ACTION

Squadron Leader Ronald Rankin and Major Stuart Peach had filed their report to the United Nations Commission on Korea only hours before the North Korean People's Army surged south in the opening volley of the war. That report formed the opening words of the United Nations Security Council's (UNSC) 25 June 1950 meeting which subsequently resolved that the attack by North Korean forces had constituted a breach of peace on the peninsula. Resolution 82, as it was known, also called for an immediate halt to hostilities and the withdrawal of North Korean forces back to the 38th Parallel. Days later, the UNSC passed a further resolution that called upon members of the United Nations (UN) to assist the Republic of Korea ward off the attack by North Korea and restore peace in the South. On 28 June, Seoul fell to North Korean forces, by which time Rankin was making his return to Japan via Pusan, ahead of the invading force.

Although already placed on standby by the United States Air Force's (USAF) Fifth Air Force, the authority for No 77 Squadron to enter the war rested with the Australian Government. As Supreme Commander of all UN forces in Korea, General Douglas MacArthur was keen to call upon the Australians and requested this of Lieutenant General Horace Robertson, the Commander-in-Chief of the British Commonwealth Occupation Force. On Friday 30 June, Prime Minister Robert Menzies and the Australian Government committed No 77 Squadron to the war.

The commitment of the Mustangs was significant as it represented nearly all of Australia's effective operational fighter strength at home and abroad. It was also important to the Fifth Air Force as the Australians were the only squadron of the type in the region; air operations over Korea from bases in Japan required an extensive range that only the famed Second World War escort fighter could provide.

The USAF F-80 Shooting Stars based in Japan could only manage 15–20 minutes over targets in Korea before they needed to return. Additionally, in the initial stages of the war, the airfields at Pusan, Taegu and Pohang possessed runways too rugged and too short to accommodate jet aircraft.

The first mission of the Korean War took place on 2 July when four Mustangs of No 77 Squadron departed Iwakuni, Japan, at dawn, led by Squadron Leader Graham Strout. The task was to provide air cover against enemy attacks over Taejon Airfield in Korea while three Douglas C-47 Dakotas landed and evacuated wounded American personnel. One Mustang returned shortly after take-off when it became unserviceable and, except for initial radio contact with the Dakotas, the Australian pilots did not see the aircraft despite holding overhead the airfield for an hour before returning to Japan. It was an uneventful commencement of operations.

Artwork by Robert Taylor depicting six RAAF Mustangs escorting nine USAF Boeing B-29 Superfortress bombers on a raid over North Korea. (Australian War Memorial)

In his Australians at War Film Archive recording, Flight Sergeant Milt Cottee recalled flying on the squadron's first mission of the Korean War with an individual first:

> Careful taxi out and take off, join up in close formation, and then into line astern to go up through the cloud. Emerged on the top of the cloud and then that Number 3 declared something wrong with his radio and went back. So that left us three. We formed up in battle formation with three, about 200 yards apart.
>
> It wasn't until the light, the sun came up, the dawn approached, that we went out into battle formation, and we were in battle formation when we saw the coast of Korea coming up. Tom Murphy was the other pilot – he was out on the right and I saw him surging forward a bit just before we came to the coast and I thought, 'What the hell are you doing, Tom?'
>
> Graham Strout called him up and said, 'How are you going, Tom?' and he didn't say anything. And then the penny dropped. He was the first one into Korea as we crossed the coast.

The second mission was led by Wing Commander Lou Spence, departing two hours after the first, with eight Mustangs to rendezvous over Korea with 17 USAF Douglas B-26 Invader bombers. The target was two bridges spanning the Han River, south of Seoul, and, on arriving, the Mustangs separated into two sections to cover the Invaders, which had split into rocketing and bombing sections respectively. The third and final mission of the first day was led by Flight Lieutenant Gordon Harvey and was another escort mission, this time for USAF Boeing B-29 Superfortress bombers.

The first day of operations had seen the squadron return unscathed with only inaccurate ground fire sighted on the second mission and medium anti-aircraft fire on the third. More than 70 hours had been flown by the squadron, but it would be the following day, 3 July, that the unit would perform its first offensive mission of the war.

Wing Commander Louis Thomas Spence DFC, Commanding Officer of No 77 Squadron, briefs his pilots before taking off on their first mission over South Korea. (Australian War Memorial)

Wing Commander Spence was to lead the mission and, before the flight, queried the target information provided by the Fifth Air Force. In a rapidly moving war, the area tasked for the attack was near the front line where opposing sides were close to each other. The target location was verified by the USAF and, at 1:59 pm, eight Mustangs, each carrying six rockets, departed Iwakuni. The objective was to strafe and rocket the road between Heitaku and Suwon, attacking any targets of opportunity they encountered.

The pilots sighted a train and a column of trucks heading south and commenced the attack. Flight Lieutenant Bay Adams was about to rocket the locomotive when he thought he had seen South Korean markings and aborted his attack. He instructed his flight to hold fire and, when he called in his position, he was assured by an American forward air control aircraft that the area was occupied by the North Koreans.

In 20 minutes over the target, the Mustangs destroyed locomotives, trucks, a staff car and rocketed a bridge. Vehicles were left ablaze, although the damage to the bridge was obscured by the pall of smoke that soon blanketed the area.

On his return to Iwakuni, Spence again sought verification of the target area and its proximity to the front line and was again reassured the area was controlled by the enemy. What appeared to be a successful first strike, however, soon became a tragedy of war. The Australians had fired upon Allied forces in a friendly fire incident with the trucks and trains carrying American and South Korean troops and ammunition.

Brigadier General Timberlake and his deputy, Lieutenant General Partridge from the Fifth Air Force Tactical Control Center at Itazuke, personally apologised to the Australians for the faulty target information. The incident was widely reported in American newspapers as a United Press journalist had been on the ground during the attack and recognised the Australian markings borne by the Mustangs. The rapid onset and escalation of the war had an impact beyond the fluid state of the front line. Command and control processes were also required to improve significantly if incidents like that of 3 July were not to be repeated.

At Iwakuni, there were concerns on the evening of 6 July when three Mustangs had not returned from a rocket attack on a bridge at Pyeongtaek. The leader, Squadron Leader Strout, had returned with an unserviceable aircraft while the other Mustangs continued to the target. Low on fuel, they had opted to land and remain overnight at Taejon airfield, where they had been met with some unfriendly American faces in the wake of the friendly fire incident. The squadron at Iwakuni was not made aware of the pilots landing safely until the next morning in another failure of communications.

A group of No 77 Squadron flight and ground crew gather informally outside their crew room. The sign on the building reads '77 FIGHTER SQUADRON' and the open area of the building (right) appears to be a canteen named 'Bonnie's Country'. The pilots are wearing lifejackets and pistols in their holsters in preparation for the squadron's first mission in support of the United Nations in South Korea. (Australian War Memorial)

On 7 July, the UNSC recommended all UN military assistance be unified under the United States; General Douglas MacArthur was appointed Commander-in-Chief of the United Nations Command. The same day, Strout led a strafing and rocketing mission against the railyards at Samcheok. Leading two Mustangs into the diving attack, the other two pilots witnessed a bright flash and believed Strout had hit a good target. A later account from a witness on the ground would state that Strout's Mustang suddenly dived towards the ground billowing black smoke and fire before breaking up in mid-air. Graham Strout was No 77 Squadron's first casualty of the Korean War. His remains would be discovered, exhumed and reburied in late December as part of a recovery mission led by RAAF Chaplain Esmond New.

As offensive operations increased, the Mustangs were consistently subjected to anti-aircraft and small-arms fire. Close support of the ground forces was a primary role for 77 Squadron throughout July and, by the second half of the month, the Mustangs were staging through Taegu as Taejon was abandoned by UN forces. Having flown out of Iwakuni in the morning, the fighters would conduct their first mission over Korea before landing at Taegu to refuel and rearm. Following their second sortie, they would return to Iwakuni for the evening where the crews of No 491 Squadron would ready the aircraft for the next morning.

The ground-attack missions armed the Mustangs with a variety of weapons in addition to their six .50-calibre machine guns; the fighters could carry two 500-lb bombs or up to ten rockets. Additionally, the Mustangs could carry drop tanks containing napalm to ignite a fire over a wider area and were effective in attacking Russian-built T-34 tanks. When the fuse failed to ignite the petroleum-based jelly, tracers could be fired by the Mustang to set the napalm off.

Japanese maintenance workers helping to prepare a Mustang for a sortie over Korea. (Australian War Memorial)

With only five years passed since the end of the war with Japan, it was an interesting development that the ground crews were assisted by Japanese technicians who had learned their skills in the previous conflict. However, now they maintained, fuelled and armed aircraft of the Royal Australian Air Force rather than the Imperial Japanese Navy, some while wearing weathered and de-badged caps and clothing of their wartime service.

Key to effective close support was the gathering of accurate and timely target intelligence. To this end, a coordinated system was provided by American airborne controllers in light aircraft to direct the strikes with precision. The Mustangs would first contact a ground controller, operating under the callsign *Mellow*, who in turn passed them to an airborne controller in the area of operations. Flying North American T-6 Texans or Piper L-3 Cubs, under the appropriate callsigns of *Dragonfly* or *Mosquito*, the controllers were in contact with ground forces by radio and could orchestrate the attack with extreme accuracy and detail. Rather than a general area to be attacked, the airborne controllers could specify the exact location of a vehicle, troop concentration or building between passes by the attacking aircraft. These instructions could be refined to a matter of hundreds of yards, relative to a notable feature, or a previous attack, while keeping the aircraft well clear of friendly ground forces.

A USAF T-6 Texan used in the forward air control role, callsign *Mosquito*. (Unknown via Dennis Newton)

The first month of operations had seen No 77 Squadron fly a total of 1,337 hours which comprised seven combat air patrol (CAP) sorties, 295 close-support sorties and 53 escort sorties. The squadron's work was not going unnoticed, receiving praise from MacArthur. As

Wirraway A20-750

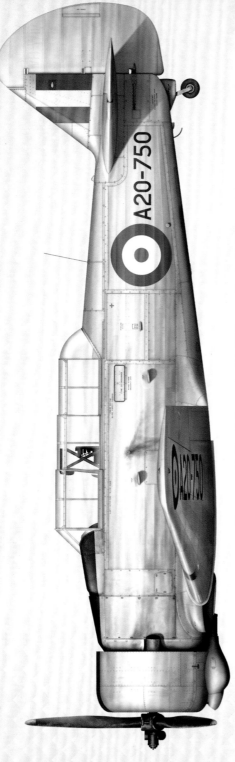

Commonwealth Aircraft Corporation CA-16 Wirraway (Juanita Franzi)

A20-750 was one of several Wirraways allocated to No 81 Wing and operated by No 77 Squadron during its service in Japan. It was written off after a forced landing on a beach at Sahaya, Japan, on 20 July 1951.

TECHNICAL DATA

DESCRIPTION:
Two-seat general purpose and advanced trainer.

POWER PLANT:
One 447-kW (600-hp) Pratt & Whitney R-1340 Wasp radial piston engine.

DIMENSIONS:
Span 13.10 m (43 ft 0 in); length 8.48 m (27 ft 10 in); height (excluding radio mast) 2.66 m (8 ft 9 in).

WEIGHTS:
Empty 1,811 kg (3,992 lb); normal loaded (trainer) 2,553 kg (5,630 lb); max loaded 2,991 kg (6,595 lb).

PERFORMANCE:
Max speed 354 km/h (220 mph); cruising speed 293 km/h (182 mph); initial climb 594 m/min (1,950 ft/min); ceiling 7,010 m (23,000 ft); range 1,158 km (720 miles).

recorded in the Commanding Officer's Report for July 1950, he advised Wing Commander Spence:

> The work of the pilots has already been highly praised by all those who have seen them in action in Korea but I would also like to commend the fine work being done by the ground crews and maintenance personnel generally all of whom are working long hours in very hot and humid conditions and are keeping the machines in first-class battle condition.

Spence was also advised the unit had won the Duke of Gloucester Cup, which was awarded to the most efficient squadron in the RAAF. A personal message of congratulations was received from the Duke of Gloucester noting that, '... the general efficiency and excellence of your squadron is bearing fruit in the highly successful operations which you are carrying out in Korea ...'

After only a month of operations, the squadron was drawing high praise from all quarters. A Cinesound crew recorded a strike in July (for Cinesound News No 983), mounting a camera in a modified drop tank beneath the wing of one of the Mustangs. A cameraman also flew in the open cockpit of the back seat of one of the squadron's CAC Wirraways at the beginning of the flight to capture air-to-air footage of the Mustangs and a C-47.

Footage showed 40,000 South Korean refugees camped in a riverbed before the Mustangs arrived at their target near Haegu and commenced the attack. Strafing and rocketing buildings and troop lines among the rugged terrain, the film also captured the aircraft recovering to Taegu where the C-47 was offloading the cargo and armaments it had conveyed. Returning to Iwakuni, the pilots were shown debriefing and the ground crews repairing and readying the Mustangs for the next day.

In the Cinesound film, Wing Commander Spence was featured away from the flight line, bidding his wife and two children farewell outside their quarters before he left for the day's mission. Returning late in the day, from the battle that would be known as the Pusan Perimeter, Spence was conveyed directly from the flight line to the mess where Lieutenant General Stratemeyer waited. Spence wore a sweat-stained uniform and the stubble upon his face was evidence of a long day in the cockpit as he was greeted by the general. He was presented with the US Legion of Merit for his leadership and the effectiveness of No 77 Squadron in the war to date.

For the family of Lou Spence, the sight of his Mustang with the red spinner returning at the end of a mission was a sight to which they had become accustomed. Having the families on base with the operational squadron flying into harm's way daily provided a polarised existence for the pilots. It was an existence that would be tested when losses began to mount in the crucible of the Pusan Perimeter, a battle that would ultimately claim the life of a highly respected and admired leader – Wing Commander Louis Thomas Spence DFC AM (US).

Lou Spence strapping into the cockpit with assistance from his ground crew. (Australian War Memorial

Chapter 4
THE PUSAN PERIMETER

August 1950 began as Prime Minister Menzies addressed both Houses of Congress in Washington while, on the Korean Peninsula, the speed of the advance southward by the North Korean forces was devastating. From the first incursion on 25 June, the North Korean People's Army (NKPA) had swept all before it as it set about its goal of the reunification of North and South Korea over the ensuing six weeks. By late August, it had confined the United Nations (UN) forces to a small corner on the south-eastern tip of the Korean Peninsula, threatening to push those same forces into the sea. This line of final resistance measured 100 miles by 50 miles (roughly 160 kilometres by 80 kilometres) and came to be known as the Pusan Perimeter.

The western perimeter was formed along the natural line of the Nakdong River which ran south to north, while the northern perimeter headed east along rugged, mountainous terrain. Within its bounds were contained the UN forces and General Walton's US Eighth Army.

The Australian flyers were in the midst of the battle, departing Iwakuni at dawn and staging through Taegu, operating under the distinctive callsign *Dropkick*, with their targets growing ever closer as the NKPA closed in on the perimeter. Although the long day was planned to conclude at Iwakuni, the aircraft and pilots would frequently remain overnight at Taegu.

Members of No 77 Squadron examine a damaged undercarriage door on a Mustang that has just returned from a mission over Korea. The pilot is Lou Spence. (Australian War Memorial)

The battle was so close at its peak that the Mustangs were attacking targets within minutes of taking off and the sounds of the ground war could be heard on the airfield. On occasion, the first flights of the day would clear the take-off and approach paths of potential ground fire from ground troops that had advanced close to the airfield boundary overnight. Three or four sorties could be flown in a day by a single pilot, each time returning to Taegu to join the queue to rearm and refuel before setting course for the battle again.

Interviewed in March 2004 for the Australians at War Film Archive, Sergeant Jim Flemming (later Air Vice-Marshal) recalled the intensity of the operations during the battle, notably the proximity of the enemy that,

> … came right down to the Pusan perimeter. We flew six missions one day … holding troops back. And one of the most horrific things I can ever recall in my life was actually firing on these things and the river was actually running red, the river was turning red from the number of bodies we were shooting in the river.

> But for the fact that we kept these people back, they would have overrun all the retreating Americans and South Koreans. But for our power they would have lost the war a lot earlier, that kept them there. But this was an awful day because all we fired at was troops.

In the defence of the Pusan Perimeter, No 77 Squadron used rockets to great effect, particularly against the columns of T-34 tanks that advanced southwards. Beyond the tanks, the Mustangs destroyed trucks, trains, and fuel and ammunition dumps as the battle reached its crescendo in late August.

Mustang on approach to land at Pusan. (Ces Sly)

Overall, August 1950 saw more than 1,700 hours flown by the 36 Mustang pilots and the lone C-47 Dakota crew that had completed training. The latter, led by Flight Lieutenant David Hitchins, flew 13 sorties to Korea that month and ferried supplies, parts and personnel into Taegu. On one flight, they carried the Chief of the Air Staff, Air Marshal George Jones, to the Korean Peninsula. For the Mustangs, there was action beyond the Pusan Perimeter as armed-reconnaissance missions took the aircraft as far north as the Russian and Manchurian borders; while flak rose from below, the enemy was yet to be encountered in the air.

On 9 September, Wing Commander Spence led four aircraft to Pusan where they were diverted by the controller, *Mellow*, to fly a close-support mission at Angang-Ni, although one aircraft landed at Pusan with engine trouble. The remaining three Mustangs were fully armed with rockets, bombs, napalm and guns, and commenced their diving attack from only 700 feet due to poor visibility and low cloud in the area. Spence was first to commence the attack and was seen to dive at an unusually steep angle before commencing a pull out so sharp that heavy vapour trails were visible streaming from the wingtips of the red-nose Mustang. The pilots then witnessed the aircraft impact the ground in the centre of the town, exploding in a mass of flame.

Sergeant Jim Flemming described the impact of the loss of Lou Spence:

> Oh gloom, nobody in the bar, no light chit chat. A terrible feeling of depression over everybody.

> Luckily we had blokes like 'Bay' Adams who was an old wartime pilot who'd been through it before and he managed to boost us all up again and say, 'That's what it's all about. It's for real so you've just got to face up to it.'

> Which we did and you start to accept losses then as a way of life.

The loss of the much-respected Spence came only a week after Bill Harrop had gone missing. Harrop had requested to leave a section covering B-29 Superfortresses when he became low on fuel. Granted permission to return to Taegu, Harrop called shortly afterwards to report he was 'going in', with his crash landing observed by the forward air controller. Harrop was seen to lay down in the field and cover himself in mud before running to a nearby hut. He would again be sighted waving from the hut when other Mustangs arrived on the scene but, when a helicopter arrived two hours later, Harrop was gone. His fate was only discovered in December by the recovery mission led by Chaplain Esmond New – shot in an exchange with North Korean soldiers.

Squadron morale suffered in the wake of the losses. Lou Spence was respected by both those who served with him and those who commanded UN operations in Korea; he was described by General Stratemeyer as, 'one of the most capable field commanders I have been associated with'. Deservedly, his leadership had earned him selection to attend Staff College in Britain in early 1951, only a matter of months away at the time of his death.

Mustang A68-809

North American P-51D Mustang (Juanita Franzi)

Wing Commander Louis 'Lou' Thomas Spence was killed in September 1950 while flying A68-809 on a ground attack mission.

TECHNICAL DATA

DESCRIPTION:
Single-seat fighter-bomber

POWER PLANT:
One 1,283-kW (1,720-hp) Packard Merlin V-1650 V12 piston engine.

DIMENSIONS:
Span 11.28 m (37 ft); length 9.83 m (32 ft 5 in); height 3.71 m (12 ft 2 in).

WEIGHTS:
Operational empty 3,567 kg (7,863 lb); normal loaded 4,309 kg (9,500 lb); max loaded 4,763 kg (10,500 lb).

ARMAMENT:
Six 0.50-in machine guns in wings; two 227-kg (500-lb) or 454-kg (1,000-lb) bombs or six 127-mm (5-in) rockets under wings.

PERFORMANCE:
Max speed 703 km/h (437 mph) at 7,620 m (25,000 ft); max climb 1,059 m/min (3,475 ft/min); service ceiling 12,771 m (41,900 ft); range (internal fuel) 1,529 km (950 miles) or 2,655 km (1,650 miles) with external tanks.

Before Korea, Spence had served with distinction during the Second World War, flying Curtiss P-40 Kittyhawks with No 3 Squadron, Royal Australian Air Force (RAAF), against the *Luftwaffe* in North Africa's Western Desert campaign. Flying ground-attack missions, but also achieving aerial victories, Spence had been awarded the Distinguished Flying Cross before returning to Australia to serve in a range of operational and training roles, including as Commanding Officer of No 452 Squadron RAAF flying Spitfires in the defence of Darwin and the North-Western Area. The end of the war saw him leave the RAAF, only to re-enlist a year later and subsequently lead No 77 Squadron during its role with the British Commonwealth Occupation Force and the outbreak of the Korean War.

Airmen from No 77 Squadron maintaining one of their Mustangs at Pusan, South Korea (Australian War Memorial)

By early September, the combination of the rapid advance of NKPA and the dogged resistance and air superiority of the UN forces at the Pusan Perimeter had left the North Korean forces stagnating and with stretched supply lines. The ability to advance further had been halted and General Douglas MacArthur saw the opportunity to reverse the tide of the war by isolating the North Koreans in the south by making an amphibious landing behind enemy lines. MacArthur had chosen Inch'ŏn as the site of the landing, a heavily defended area prone to substantial tides of up to 11 metres. Named Operation *Chromite*, it was to be the first landing of its type since the Second World War and was met with resistance by some senior military stakeholders due to the potential difficulty in making it successful.

Significant planning and preparations were undertaken in the weeks preceding the landing, including a diversionary bombardment on Kunsan to deflect attention from Inch'ŏn as a possible point of landing. Following bombardment from sea and air, the amphibious assault was launched early on the morning of 15 September, taking the North Koreans by surprise. Over the following days, the UN forces fought to reclaim Seoul and the important airfield at Kimpo. A week after the landing, the airfield was being used by UN aircraft, while the US Marines had brought ashore more than 6,000 vehicles and 50,000 personnel.

In the south, General Walker's Eighth Army broke out of the Pusan Perimeter and, by 22 September, had the NKPA in retreat and caught between Walker and the US Marines that had landed at Inch'ŏn. Walker's break-out was the beginning of a counteroffensive that would see the UN forces push north, with MacArthur authorising operations north of the 38th Parallel on 27 September.

A Korean armourer wearing a belt of 0.5-inch ammunition at Taegu. (Australian War Memorial)

The breakout from the Pusan Perimeter also changed the role of No 77 Squadron. Having previously flown to defend the perimeter, they now flew north in support of the advancing UN ground forces. Attacking supply lines, communication and railway systems, and retreating troops, the Mustangs now flew deep into North Korea as far as the 40th Parallel. Without air opposition, wireless jamming or anti-aircraft fire, the close-support missions proved to be very successful. Whereas operations from Taegu had been flown against targets close to the Pusan Perimeter, and were sometimes measured in minutes, the flights north could see the pilots in their cockpits for upwards of six hours.

Led by their new commanding officer, Squadron Leader 'Dick' Cresswell, pilots study a target map prior to taking off to attack North Korean forces. (Australian War Memorial)

Coinciding with the breakout from the Pusan Perimeter, the squadron received a new commanding officer to replace Lou Spence. Squadron Leader Richard 'Dick' Cresswell had commanded the squadron in Australia shortly after its formation in Pearce, Western Australia, in 1942 and had famously destroyed a Mitsubishi G4M 'Betty' bomber in the defence of Darwin on 23 November 1942. This was recognised as the first aerial victory by an Australian squadron over the mainland. Cresswell took the unit to New Guinea in May of the following year before handing over command in August.

He returned to New Guinea in September 1944 and once again commanded No 77 Squadron before becoming Wing Leader with No 81 Wing in December, having effectively held both positions since his arrival. Returning to Australia in 1945, Cresswell served in a variety of roles with the RAAF post-war. These included developing a Mustang conversion course to train pilots bound for service in Japan with Nos 76, 77 and 82 Squadrons.

When the call came for Cresswell to take command in Korea, it was a unique situation as he became the only officer to command the same squadron three times in wartime. However, decades later, when interviewed for the Australians at War Film Archive in September 2003, he would recall:

> It was a nasty bloody war, too. Cruel. Dangerous. The weapons we were using, like Napalm, the type of targets we were hitting. Trains, tunnels, troop concentrations. Tanks.

> It was a closer war than World War II as far as I'm concerned. ... Korea was a very different, and very ugly, war.

FLIGHT LIEUTENANT
DAVID HITCHINS

David Hitchins enlisted in the Royal Australian Air Force (RAAF) in 1942 and, having trained as a pilot, converted to the DAP Beaufort torpedo bomber. He served with No 100 Squadron RAAF at Milne Bay, New Guinea, and was tasked with bombing missions against both maritime and land targets. Following the end of the war in the Pacific, Hitchins first flew the C-47 Dakota with No 33 Squadron in Townsville before the squadron was disbanded. He was then posted to Port Moresby flying air-sea rescue before that unit was disbanded in 1947.

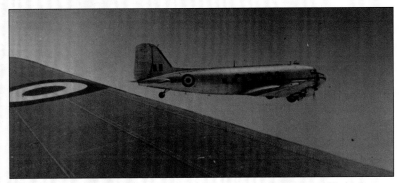

Two Dakotas of No 30 Transport Unit in formation over Korea. (David Hitchins)

Hitchins first flew out of Iwakuni with No 1315 Flight RAF in 1947, operating the Dakota, before being posted to No 77 Squadron as the commander of the Communications Flight's two C-47s. When the Korean War broke out in June 1950, Hitchins initially commanded No 30 Communication Unit until the arrival of Squadron Leader John Gerber in January 1952. During the Battle of the Pusan Perimeter, Hitchins flew numerous dangerous missions through the Taegu Valley to support No 77 Squadron. He also served as the personal VIP pilot of the Commander-in-Chief of United Nations Forces, Lieutenant General Sir Horace Robertson.

David Hitchins with one of the Austers of No 30 Communication Unit. (David Hitchins)

When Hitchins left for Australia in May 1951, he had been in Japan for more than four years and flown more than 100 missions to Korea and 1,500 hours in the Dakota. Squadron Leader Gerber was high in praise for his predecessor whose contribution had been substantial.

On his return to Australia, Hitchins held several postings, including serving as Governor-General Sir William Slim's personal pilot and being posted to Great Britain. Formerly No 30 Communication Unit/No 30 Transport Unit, Hitchins's old unit reformed as No 36 Squadron and in 1964 he took command of the squadron as a wing commander and served during the Vietnam conflict.

Flight Lieutenant David Hitchins on the occasion of his marriage in Japan to Flight Officer Jean Mills of the RAAF Nursing Service. (David Hitchins)

David Hitchins ultimately rose to the rank of air commodore and served his final posting as the Officer Commanding RAAF Pearce in Western Australia.

Chapter 5
NORTH TO THE YALU RIVER

The aftermath of the Inch'ŏn landings in September 1950 saw the rapid advance northward of the United Nations (UN) forces with the Republic of Korea 3rd Infantry Division crossing the 38th Parallel. However, a long-held concern was apparent regarding Korea's northern neighbour, China. In Peking, the Premier of the People's Republic of China, Zhou Enlai, had warned the Indian Ambassador that if the Americans crossed the 38th Parallel, China would enter the war.

Despite the warning, the UN General Assembly authorised United Nations Command (UNC) Forces to pursue the North Korean People's Army north beyond the 38th Parallel. In response, 300,000 troops of the Chinese People's Volunteer Army began to cross the Yalu River, south into North Korea.

Keeping pace with the advance, No 77 Squadron had moved its base north to remain within a manageable reach of the front line and beyond. Arriving on 12 October, its new home was K3 airfield at Pohang on the east coast of South Korea. Operating from Pohang reduced the return journey by hundreds of miles, allowing the Mustangs to fly even deeper into North Korea on their interdiction missions, destroying roads, railways, trucks and supply lines.

With the approaching winter making its presence felt, ground crew arm a Mustang with napalm drop tanks.
(Australian War Memorial)

The C-47 Dakotas ferried in supplies and tents to establish the new base at Pohang as the harsh weather began to turn with the arrival of November. The airfield possessed no apron area but had significant areas of mud and a short runway, which again meant the Mustang was the only suitable aircraft to operate under conditions that ruled out jet fighters.

As the squadron was settling in at Pohang, No 91 Wing came into being under the command of Group Captain A Dallas Charlton. Aside from No 77 Squadron, the new wing consisted of No 391 Base Squadron, No 491 Maintenance Squadron and No 30 Communication Unit (later renamed No 30 Transport Unit). The latter's two Dakotas were soon joined by more from Australia and No 38 Squadron in Malaya, bringing the strength to seven by the close of 1950.

As well as supporting No 77 Squadron, the communications unit flew multiple 'Army courier' flights to deliver supplies and reinforcements to P'yŏngyang as the battle front continued to move north. The pace was such that No 77 Squadron was already looking to move further north to Yonpo, south of Hamhŭng, in North Korea; the Dakotas began positioning the advance party to nearby K-27 early in November.

At Pohang, a work party of Australians and Koreans from No 77 Squadron push a jeep into a C-47 Dakota of No 30 Communication Unit. (Australian War Memorial)

As plans for the move were being made, there were still opportunities to maintain morale, through Melbourne Cup sweepstakes and four pilots flying to Iwakuni to participate in the British Commonwealth Occupation Force (BCOF) tennis championships. However, there was no escaping that the brutal cold of the squadron's first Korean winter. Pohang provided challenges, such as living under canvas and servicing the aircraft in sub-zero conditions. Ground crews were exposed to the elements as they battled to ready the Mustangs for their next day's flying. Despite the best efforts of the Dakotas, winter clothing was scarce with summer uniforms being worn in conjunction with American equipment that could be sourced, scavenged or traded.

The ongoing shortage had fatal consequences for two pilots in mid-November. With a primitive wiring arrangement supplying power to the tents, a fault ignited the one shared by Flight Lieutenants Craig Kirkpatrick and William Gray. As the tent flared into a blaze, the two pilots had difficulty escaping their sleeping bags and emerged on fire. Sadly, both men succumbed to their burns.

The squadron continued to attack enemy troops, trucks and installations in an armed-reconnaissance role and flew close support for the advancing Allied ground forces, including Australian troops for the first time. Of their close air support of the Royal Australian Regiment (3rd Battalion), Major Ian B Ferguson described it as '… an all-Australian day', with '… the closest air support I have ever seen'.

With shades of the friendly fire incident in July, the squadron was called in to strike suspected enemy troops who responded to their approach by walking into the open and waving. The Mustangs held their fire and queried the instruction; when no confirmation was forthcoming, they were redirected to confirmed enemy troops elsewhere, to find them burrowed into a series of foxholes.

The state of the war was flowing in favour of the UN forces and, in some quarters, there was confidence the war would soon be over. As far back as October 1950, General MacArthur had expressed to President Truman, 'I believe that formal resistance will end throughout North and South Korea by Thanksgiving' and 'It is my hope to be able to withdraw the Eighth Army to Japan by Christmas.' Even so, as the general and the president spoke, China was increasing its presence in the war with troops moving into North Korea, travelling by night and generally undetected (other than the few taken prisoner). Still, by mid-November, the confidence of MacArthur had grown even greater, although ominous signs had begun to surface.

The Yalu River was far more than a major geographical feature, its winding path marking the border between North Korea and Manchuria; it was a political line in the sand. To this backdrop, MacArthur's push north beyond the 38th Parallel did not sit well with Truman and, when the general suggested bombing targets in Manchuria, the president mandated that no bombing occur within five miles south of the Yalu River.

This offered the Chinese build-up north of the Yalu River immunity from attack. However, UN aircraft had already been fired at from north of the Yalu and air bases in Manchuria were being developed, with the appearance of new swept-wing jet fighters at Antung airfield, just north of the Yalu. The first contact with these aircraft had occurred on 1 November when six Mikoyan-Gurevich MiG-15s bearing Chinese markings engaged a flight of American

F-51 Mustangs to the south of the Yalu. This action accelerated the United States Air Force's (USAF) introduction of the North American F-86A Sabre into the theatre, another swept-wing jet of comparable performance.

The MiG-15 had a significant speed advantage over the first-generation UN jets, such as the F-80 Shooting Star and the F-84 Thunderjet, and heralded an end to the air superiority the UN air forces had enjoyed. In its place would emerge a patch of airspace over North Korea to the south of the Yalu River that would become synonymous with air-to-air engagements between jet adversaries – 'MiG Alley'.

A jeep parked and maintenance tent on a snow-covered apron at K-27, an airfield previously used by the North Korean Air Force, between Yonpo and Hamhŭng on the east coast of North Korea. (Australian War Memorial)

For the Royal Australian Air Force (RAAF), operations from K-27 Hamhŭng commenced on 20 November and were very close to the front line in North Korea. The accommodation needed some repairs but was of brick construction with wooden floors and soon hot showers were operational. Airfield defence was organised and all personnel were instructed to be armed at all times as enemy guerilla activity was expected. Again, the runway was short and the freezing conditions made icy taxiways and runways another hazard to overcome. The ground crews again battled through trying conditions where a tool could become frozen to an airframe or, worse, to an ungloved hand on contact.

Despite observing the presence of the Chinese build-up of MiG fighters, the presence of massed Chinese troops had apparently escaped MacArthur's notice (or he ignored the threat they posed). Consequently, on the night of 25-26 November, more than 200,000 Chinese troops attacked the 30,000 soldiers of the US Eighth Army north of the Ch'ŏngch'ŏn River, inflicting heavy casualties.

The next day, No 77 Squadron went into action at maximum effort, flying 21 close-support missions to '… stem the breakthrough in the Chosin Reservoir area', as Squadron Leader Cresswell would explain in his report. Cresswell would also draw attention to the ground crew who 'did the most amazing job in keeping the aircraft operational'. He highlighted the extreme conditions under which they worked, with the coldest day, –23 degrees Celsius, occurring days after the Chosin Reservoir battle commenced.

Armed with napalm-filled drop tanks, Ian 'Pip' Olorenshaw prepares for a mission from Ay Hamhŭng.
(Australian War Memorial)

The Battle of Chosin Reservoir was yet another turning point in the see-sawing conflict in Korea that transformed a seeming victory for the UN forces into another rapid withdrawal to the south. Major General Oliver P. Smith, commanding the encircled 1st Marine Division would famously describe the withdrawal by stating, 'Retreat, hell! We're not retreating, we're just advancing in a different direction.'

In Tokyo, MacArthur announced Korea was now an 'entirely new war' and, in Washington, President Truman addressed a press conference and advised that the United States would take 'whatever steps were necessary' to stop the communist advance. When pressed by another reporter whether this would include the atomic bomb, Truman replied, 'That includes every weapon that we have.'

In Korea, No 77 Squadron continued to fly close air support through the battle and on one mission escorted an American C-47 engaged in a psychological-warfare mission dropping leaflets and calling upon Chinese guerillas to surrender to UN troops. By the beginning of December, the squadron was ordered to move south to the airfield at K9 Pusan East in the region from which it had broken the Pusan Perimeter only a few months before.

On 1 December, K-27 was blanketed in snow as two Mustangs set course for Iwakuni, to inform Group Captain Charlton of the impending move south, and two USAF C-46 Commando transports departed with personnel and supplies bound for K9. The next day, two RAAF Dakotas from No 30 Communication Unit were inbound from Iwakuni and began the transfer of supplies to Pusan East. The Unit History relates an unending stream of aircraft came and went from Hamhŭng as smoke rolled down from the direction of the Chosin Reservoir. As each Mustang departed, it did so fully armed and conducted a close-support mission before turning south for K9. The final departure from Hamhŭng was a section of four, led by Cresswell. The four Mustangs attacked both ends of a tunnel concealing troops before striking a village and vehicles and setting course for Pusan.

Pusan East, since it was called K9, was more colloquially known as 'Dogpatch'. The living conditions were good with proper barracks accommodation and US food provisioned. As personnel were still arriving, pilots refuelled and rearmed their aircraft in the absence of ground crew. Despite the move, operations continued unabated, and Cresswell reported morale remained high, partially aided by the news the squadron was to receive replacements for the Mustangs in the form of the British Gloster Meteor F.8 twin-engine jet fighter. An initial order for 36 single-seat F.8 Meteors and four T.7 two-seat trainers had been placed with the British Government.

Operations from Dogpatch were hampered by difficulty in locating targets among the snow-covered terrain which also impeded navigation. Close-support missions were flown for the withdrawing troops but targets for armed-reconnaissance missions became more difficult to find. Notably, the Chinese advance was heavily supported by oxen and other animals in the absence of motorised vehicles and many of these fell alongside the troops when they came under attack. This also represented a shift in operations for the squadron as the Chinese moved south and their lines of supply became longer and more vulnerable. A campaign of interdiction emerged that had not existed when the battle front was nearer the Yalu River and supplies were forthcoming over the short distance from the safety of Manchuria.

By mid-December, it was reported that 400,000 Chinese troops were confronting UNC forces as they moved south beyond the 38th Parallel once again. On the 23rd, the US was dealt a blow. Lieutenant General Walton Walker, a veteran of both world wars who had led the US Eighth Army through the dark days of the Pusan Perimeter and led the breakout to the north as far as the Yalu, was killed when his jeep collided with a South Korean weapons carrier.

As the battle raged through Christmas, a lesser-known struggle was taking place. RAAF Chaplain Squadron Leader Desmond New had served as a chaplain during the Second World War and as an intelligence officer with the Special Duties Branch BCOF in Japan following the war. New was fluent in Japanese and Korean and familiar with the intricacies of their respective cultures. He was tasked with locating and recovering the bodies of two missing pilots, Squadron Leader Graham Strout and Pilot Officer Bill Harrop.

Arriving in Korea on Christmas Day, New was accompanied by Sergeant Tom Henderson, a Second World War veteran of RAAF search-and-rescue in New Guinea, and a small party of South Korean commandos. Trekking up the east coast and then south to Waegwan on the Nakdong River in search of the downed airmen, the party was fired at by communist guerillas, frostbitten, and exposed to the brutal winter weather. Both airmen were located and recovered and laid to rest where the United Nations Memorial Cemetery stands today at Busan. Air Commodore Alan M Charlesworth, Chief of Staff Headquarters BCOF, and Squadron Leader Cresswell attended the service for the two fighter pilots.

The squadron operated through Christmas and into the New Year without pause. For those not in the air, a sumptuous Christmas meal of turkey, vegetables, fruit pie, beer and sweets was enjoyed. There was a sense among the squadron that a 'big move' by the Chinese could take place on Christmas Day, but it did not eventuate beyond the pace southward they had already established.

The final days of 1950 were characterised by poor weather and extreme cold. It had been a year that had seen the squadron pivot days before returning to Australia, having completed their service with the BCOF, to being one of the first units into action at the outbreak of the Korean War. On New Year's Eve, the final comment in the squadron history relates that the occasion was 'celebrated by most members of the squadron, plenty of fun and games.'

MiG ALLEY

The name 'MiG Alley' became synonymous with the first jet war. In a small wedge of sky, bordered to the north by the Yalu River, the first generation of jets duelled for air superiority.

'MiG Alley'.

In October 1950, a USAF Boeing RB-29 reconnaissance aircraft spotted 75 swept-wing jet fighters at Antung airfield to the north of the Yalu River in Manchuria. On 1 November, six of these fighters, bearing Chinese markings, engaged a flight of American F-51 Mustangs. The aircraft was the Mikoyan-Gurevich MiG-15 and was a technological leap forward from the piston-engine Yak-7 and Yak-11 aircraft that had previously been the North Koreans' front-line fighters.

The MiG-15s shot down two Boeing B-29 Superfortresses in November 1950, prompting the Americans to expedite the introduction of the North American F-86A Sabre into the Korean conflict in December to counter the new threat.

The two aircraft were similar in appearance, although the MiG was smaller and lighter than the Sabre and prone to being unstable at high speeds. The MiG was more heavily armed than the Sabre with two 23-mm and one 37-mm cannon compared to the six .50-calibre machine guns of its American adversary.

At first, the better-trained and experienced American pilots had the edge over the Chinese pilots flying the MiGs, boasting a kill ratio of 10:1. In time, this ratio became far more even as a new wave of competent pilots appeared in the enemy cockpits. Colloquially known by the Americans as 'Honchos', these pilots were soon identified as Russians, many of whom had flown in the Second World War. However, it would be 40 years before this fact was officially acknowledged by the Soviets.

A MiG-15, blowing exhaust, under attack as seen from the gun camera footage of a United Nations fighter over the mountains of Korea. (Australian War Memorial)

The geography of MiG Alley also had an impact on the conduct of the fighting. MiG Alley was 200 miles from the United Nations' (UN) bases at Kimpo and Suwon, leaving the Sabres with only 20 minutes of fighting time before they needed to return. By comparison, the MiGs could remain on the ground at Antung until the Sabres neared MiG Alley, taking flight and engaging the enemy before returning north of the Yalu River where UN aircraft could not pursue them.

No 77 Squadron first became entangled in MiG Alley in August 1951, following the introduction of the Meteor. In conducting bomber escorts and fighter sweeps, the straight-wing Meteor was outclassed by the swept-wing MiG-15 which, with the Sabre, represented the next step in the evolution of jet fighters. The loss of three RAAF aircraft to MiGs in an air battle on 1 December 1951 effectively saw the withdrawal of the Meteor from MiG Alley and led them to serve in the ground-attack role, in which No 77 Squadron established a formidable reputation.

The Korean War saw the making of numerous fighter aces on both sides of the conflict with most gaining their victories in the small patch of sky over North Korea known as MiG Alley.

Chapter 6
FINAL MONTHS OF THE MUSTANG

The dawn of 1951 saw Seoul evacuated by United Nations Command forces as a United Nations Ceasefire Group proposed five principles for an armistice in Korea, which the Chinese subsequently rejected. For No 77 Squadron, the new year heralded the sunset for their Mustang fighters, but there were still significant operations to be flown.

No 30 Communication Unit flew missions carrying reinforcements and, on 16 January, flew the first medical-evacuation flight (medevac), carrying five stretcher cases and 19 British and Australian walking wounded. Such medical evacuations by the unit were to become a pivotal role and one in which the unit would prove prolific, carrying nearly 13,000 wounded troops by the end of the war.

Mustangs of No 77 Squadron with a Dakota of No 86 Transport Wing in the foreground at K14 Kimpo.
(Australian War Memorial)

January 19 saw the squadron tasked with attacking buildings suspected of being Chinese Army Headquarters in the North Korean capital of P'yŏngyang. Twelve Mustangs, led by Dick Cresswell, attacked the target whose anti-aircraft gunners were at the ready due to a United States Air Force (USAF) B-29 bombing raid that had been executed by radar through the dense cloud cover. Ground fire was heavy, and the results of the attack were difficult for the pilots to confirm through the dust, smoke and fire beneath the cloud.

The second wave of the attack was led by Flight Lieutenant Gordon Harvey, who had been the first pilot to complete 100 missions, who calmly called that he had been hit and his engine was losing power. Two Mustangs followed his descent and observed Harvey execute a wheels-up landing on an island in the frozen Taedong River. The next morning, Cresswell led four Mustangs on a search-and-rescue mission and found Harvey's Mustang with its fuselage burnt out, the wings intact and multiple footprints surrounding the wreckage. Harvey had survived the landing unscathed but had been promptly captured on leaving his aircraft, becoming the first RAAF prisoner of war in the Korean War.

In a war that had fluctuated at such a pace, the decision of General Matthew Ridgeway to launch another counteroffensive and push north in late January followed the pattern that had evolved. Ridgeway had replaced Walker as the commander of the US Eighth Army. Named Operation *Thunderbolt*, it saw No 77 Squadron fly in a Group Exercise for the first time when 12 Mustangs joined 27 aircraft of the 39th and 40th Fighter Squadrons of the USAF. The combined effort set alight ten villages in the Yangpyeong area. The mission was led by Flight Lieutenant Ian 'Pip' Olorenshaw as Cresswell and Flight Lieutenant Des Murphy had left for Iwakuni to undertake jet training with the USAF in anticipation of the arrival of the Meteors.

The United Nations (UN) forces were once again advancing north and the Mustangs flew close-support and armed-reconnaissance missions. Notably, the squadron became effective truck hunters in their interdiction role, although this came with inherent risk from ground fire. In mid-February, a congratulatory communique was received from the Fifth Air Force for a record number of vehicles being destroyed on the 13th. In turn, the enemy had taken to concealing vehicles by driving them inside houses and creating a false wall behind them.

Flight Lieutenants Ross Coburn and Fred Barnes were the next pilots to pass 100 missions flown, sadly coinciding with the loss of Flight Lieutenant Keith Matthews and Warrant Officer Sinclair Squiers near P'yŏngyang. Both pilots were newly arrived in Korea and were returning from a mission that had been aborted due to adverse weather. Climbing through thick cloud, both subsequently went missing with the only radio transmission heard being, 'I am spinning and am going to bale out.'

The danger from ground fire was exacerbated by flak traps – decoy targets in the form of trucks and tanks to draw the fighters down into an area heavily defended by anti-aircraft emplacements. The Mustangs established a technique that involved two aircraft remaining at 3,000 feet to spot and suppress enemy fire as the other two aircraft flew in low at 300 feet to attack. Operations had proven costly in recent weeks as the squadron had lost four pilots: Flight Lieutenant Keith Matthews, Warrant Officer 'Syd' Squiers, Sergeant Ken Royal and Sergeant Harry Strange.

A Mustang, with both side panels of the windscreen shattered by a bullet, sits in a hangar waiting for repair. Flying Officer AK Frost had a lucky escape when this bullet narrowly missed him as he dived low to attack an enemy truck. (Australian War Memorial)

Testament to the effectiveness of the North Korean anti-aircraft fire, Sergeant Jim Flemming explained there were different forms of flak:

> You have 23mm which is an inch roughly and that makes a pretty fair mess of you if you get clobbered by them and they will go pretty high. 27 mm and they come up and they make a puff. They used to say during the war that you could almost walk on the flak, well in the air it was a bit like that. The whole sky just became covered with white puffs of bullets exploding and they would come to about from memory about 4 or 5,000 feet something like that.

> The big one was the 88mm radar predicted proximity fuse. You would be flying along and their radar picks you up and they assess your speed, your height and that sort of stuff and then they predict where you are going to be and then they fire off this big 88mm and it comes up and is supposed to intercept you and then it goes off at the height selected.

> They are able to nominate the height at which it goes off and it's so damn powerful that if it's within a hundred foot of you it's likely to blow you out of the air.

Sergeant 'Ces' Sly narrowly escaped capture after baling out of his Mustang on 20 March 1951. (Ces Sly)

By mid-March, the communist forces had been driven north of the Han River and the US Eighth Army had retaken Seoul. On the 20th, a notable episode in No 77 Squadron history took place when Sergeant Cecil Sly was shot down by ground fire. Sly was leading a section of two on an armed reconnaissance when his wingman, Sergeant Keith Meggs, noticed Sly's Mustang was streaming coolant from the engine. Climbing to 3,000 feet, the aircraft then caught fire and, with the cockpit filling with smoke, Sly decided to bale out of the stricken machine. With his aircraft now descending through 1,500 feet, Sly climbed out of the cockpit, although his parachute initially caught on the Mustang's canopy that he had forgotten to jettison. Seconds later, he was tumbling free, striking the tailplane as he fell.

Descending beneath his parachute, shots rang out and bullets whizzed past before he touched down and took shelter not far from his burning aircraft. The enemy was dug in all around him but was directing their fire at the successive waves of Mustangs overhead that arrived to provide cover for their downed pilot. Twenty minutes later, an American helicopter attempted a rescue and got to within 50 feet of the ground before being repelled by intense ground fire that left it severely damaged.

A USAF T-6 spotter aircraft flew overhead, tracking Sly's movements as he avoided capture and directing rescue attempts. The spotter remained on station, despite the observer being shot through the leg. It would be two hours after Sly had baled out before a second helicopter defied the odds and affected a rescue. Its pilot, Lynden E Thomason, would be credited with hundreds of rescues during his time in Korea and was awarded the Silver Star for his actions in rescuing the Australian. During his time on the ground, the Mustang pilot had been scrambling along a riverbed, hiding behind rocks and evading the best efforts of the enemy to capture or kill him. Sly was later awarded the Distinguished Flying Medal and the US Air Medal for his coolness under fire.

Although the arrival of April marked the final month for the squadron's Mustang operations, there was no reduction in effort. Flying 20 missions or more each day, they continued to strike the enemy's front line and main supply route, cutting roads and destroying bridges. The final operations took place on 6 April before the Mustangs departed Dogpatch the next day for the last time. Bound for Iwakuni, the Mustangs departed the airfield in a squadron formation. They had been thrust into the Korean War in the first days of the conflict. Their range and ability to operate from short, rough airstrips, and the pilots' experience and ongoing training during their tenure with the British Commonwealth Occupation Force, marked them as a rare resource in the theatre of operations when war broke out in July 1950. By the cessation of Mustang operations in April 1951, thirteen pilots had either been killed or listed as missing and 16 aircraft had been lost. Nearly 5,000 operational sorties had been flown, accumulating more than 11,000 hours of flight time. The squadron had claimed more than 2,300 buildings, 600 vehicles and 13 bridges and tunnels destroyed, along with a list of trains, ammunition dumps, villages, and aircraft on the ground.

The Australians' performance had been recognised at the highest levels of United Nations Command and the USAF's Fifth Air Force with one pilot receiving the Legion of Merit, and 13 US Distinguished Flying Crosses and 48 Air Medals being awarded across the squadron. Commonwealth decorations included a Bar to Wing Commander Spence's Distinguished Flying Cross, a further five Distinguished Flying Crosses and two Distinguished Flying Medals.

An armourer is using a steel rod to clean the 0.50-inch gun barrels as a young Korean assistant observes.
(Australian War Memorial)

Operating under extreme weather conditions of snow and ice, and at times living close to the battle's front line, No 77 Squadron's continual ability to achieve maximum effort in multiple roles was due to the support of the ground crews from No 491 Maintenance Squadron; as noted by Squadron Leader Cresswell, this was done without complaint.

The appearance of the MiG-15 jet fighters and the introduction of the F-86 Sabre by the USAF ushered in a new era of aerial combat. It was an era in which the disparity of speed meant the time had come for the Mustangs to be replaced; the Gloster Meteor had been chosen. The first Meteors were already at Iwakuni, having arrived by ship weeks earlier. Three days after the squadron had flown in from Pusan, lectures on the Meteor and its systems commenced.

The conversion of pilots and ground crews would take months and it would not be until late July 1951 that the squadron flew in action again. When it did, it was a very different air war.

Chapter 7
ENTER THE METEOR

The emergence of the Russian MiG-15 in Korean skies changed the face of the air war with immediate effect. While the Lockheed F-80 Shooting Star had held superiority over the few piston-engine fighters the North Korean Air Force could muster, the MiG-15 represented the next generation of jet fighter and rendered the F-80 all but obsolete in air-to-air combat. The swept-wing aircraft was a manoeuvrable fighter operating just under the speed of sound and with a 70-knot advantage over the straight-wing F-80. The other jet in the United States Air Force (USAF) arsenal was the Republic F-84 Thunderjet, which was faster than the F-80 but still inferior to the MiG-15 in a dogfight.

Gloster Meteor F.8 A77-911. (via Owen Zupp)

The only Allied aircraft positioned to challenge the MiG-15's superiority was the North American F-86A Sabre. Like the MiG, the Sabre was of the next generation of fighter jets with swept wings and it was rushed to Korea following the appearance of the MiG-15. The Sabre was slightly larger and possessed a greater top speed at lower altitudes around 25,000 feet, while the MiG was superior at high altitude. Most significantly, when two squadrons of Sabres were delivered to the 4th Fighter Interceptor Wing (FIW) in December 1950, it was estimated that, by comparison, the Chinese had 400 MiG-15s.

For the Royal Australian Air Force (RAAF), it had also become apparent the Mustang was outdated and, equally, would not meet the requirements as a component of Australia's future air-defence system. The need for a jet fighter was both essential and immediate and this was re-affirmed by Lieutenant General Stratemeyer, the Commanding General of the Far East

Air Force, when he met with Lieutenant General Robertson, Commander-in-Chief, British Commonwealth Forces, Korea, in mid-November 1950. Stratemeyer also highlighted that there was a shortage of available Sabres so Australia might need to turn elsewhere.

The British contenders for the jet-fighter role were the single-engine de Havilland DH100 Vampire and the twin-engine Gloster Meteor F.8. In early December 1950, the Australian Government under Sir Robert Menzies considered a proposal to acquire the Meteor, citing a recommendation that it was superior to the Vampire. Furthermore, with the decision being time critical, the British Government had agreed to deliver Meteor F.8s and a pair of two-seat T.7 trainers that had already been earmarked for a Royal Air Force (RAF) squadron, making them available by January. The £2.5 million order for 36 Meteor fighters and four trainers was approved by Cabinet and officially announced on 9 December.

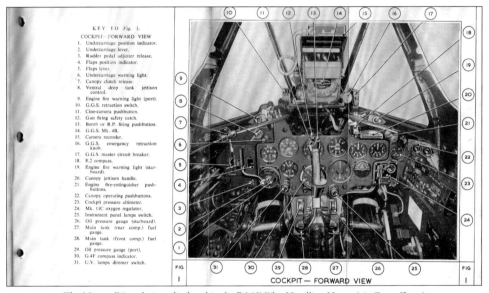

The Meteor F.8 cockpit as displayed in the RAAF Pilot Handling Notes. (via Owen Zupp)

The acquisition of the Meteor was recognised as an advancement on the Mustang but came with reservations when compared to the MiG-15. The Meteor F.8 had evolved from a Second World War design and represented the first generation of jet fighters with the lower speed and manoeuvrability associated with a straight wing. Furthermore, defining the role in which the Meteor could be used was limited as the aircraft was not designed to carry bombs and, at the time, was not approved by the RAF to fire rockets. By default, the Meteor was destined for an air-superiority role, rather than close support and armed reconnaissance, placing No 77 Squadron in direct conflict with the MiGs.

To expedite delivery of the Meteors, they were flown from the United Kingdom to Singapore where they were loaded on a Royal Navy light aircraft carrier and shipped to Iwakuni as deck cargo. The aircraft were covered in a soluble protective grease and their engine intakes and exhausts covered and sealed to protect them against the salt water and exposure of the ocean voyage.

The first load of Meteors, which included 15 F.8 fighters and two T.7 twin-seat trainers, parked on the flight deck of the light aircraft carrier HMS *Warrior* as the ship arrives in Japan in early February 1951. (Australian War Memorial)

The Meteors were assigned the prefix A77 in RAAF service, although some aircraft ultimately flew operationally in their RAF markings until they were converted. The first delivery consisted originally of 17 single-seat fighters and the four two-seat trainers. However, the Meteor destined to become A77-300 went missing over the Persian Gulf on the ferry flight to Singapore. The remaining 16 aircraft arrived at Iwakuni in late February with the balance of the initial order of 36 arriving in two later shipments in March and May.

The first Meteors arrived with narrow intakes for their Rolls-Royce Derwent engines. Cresswell was aware of 'large diameter intakes' which offered up to 200lb (91kg) extra thrust and higher speeds as a result. Consequently, the larger intakes were shipped to Iwakuni and retrofitted to the Meteors until subsequent aircraft arrived in late 1952 with the larger intakes already fitted.

In preparation for pilot training, Squadron Leader Cresswell and Flight Lieutenant Des Murphy had been assigned to the USAF's 8th Fighter Bomber Wing to gain jet experience flying the F-80 Shooting Star. Flight Lieutenant Gordon Harvey was also scheduled to join the pair but had been shot down on 19 January. Cresswell and Murphy both flew ten combat missions in the F-80 before returning to Iwakuni where the Meteors had arrived along with four RAF pilots to conduct conversion training. One of the pilots was Flight Lieutenant Max Scannell, a New Zealander on exchange with the RAF, and all four flew Mustang combat missions with No 77 Squadron during March before the unit moved to Iwakuni for conversion to the Meteor.

Ground instruction extended beyond the aircraft systems, cockpit checks and engine handling associated with the Meteor. Pilots were also lectured on the physiological aspects of high-speed and high-altitude flight. Additional lectures covered instrument flying and navigation as pilots arriving in Korea were confronted with weather conditions and snow-covered terrain for which their training in Australia had not prepared them.

Unloading a Meteor F.8 in Japan. (Australian War Memorial)

Jet operations would also see the aircraft flying at altitudes where winds were potentially far stronger, making navigation even more difficult. In his time flying the F-80 with the USAF, Creswell had experienced the benefits of an onboard radio-navigation system which allowed the pilot to home in on a ground-based beacon in all kinds of weather. Known as an Automatic Direction Finder (ADF), or colloquially as a radio compass, the USAF required the Meteor to be fitted with the navigation aid before it could participate in operations over Korea. The ADF was fitted to the Meteors at Iwakuni and was readily identified by the clear housing, in which the aerial was contained, on top of the rear fuselage. Cresswell also organised for the pilots to be instructed in making ground-controlled approaches (GCA) in which a radar controller on the ground gave headings and descents to be flown to the runway.

Accurate navigation was of increased importance due to the limited safe endurance of the Meteor, which was only about an hour using internal fuel tanks alone and dependent upon the type of operation. The Meteor could be fitted with external fuel tanks beneath the wings, outboard of the engines; however, when rocket rails were fitted in this position, fuel tanks could not be carried. A single ventral, or 'belly', tank could be carried centrally beneath the fuselage; this was used extensively although the tank was potentially vulnerable to ground fire.

As the Australians trained in earnest, a major development took place in the United Nations Command when President Truman arranged a replacement for General MacArthur who had been making public statements that contradicted the administration's policies. The new Commander-in-Chief was General Matthew Ridgeway.

A formal group portrait of No 77 Squadron pilots taken in front of one of the new Meteors. (Australian War Memorial)

Left to right: Back Row: 031569 Flying Officer KJ (Ken) Blight, A33283 Sergeant KR (Keith) Meggs, A22140 Sergeant AJ (Al) Avery, A11389 Warrant Officer RCA (Bob) Hunt, 022058 Flying Officer RW (Dick) Wittman, 033260 Flying Officer RE (Ray) Trebilco, A11412 Warrant Officer WS (Bill) Michelson, A22223 Sergeant RD (Ron) Mitchell, A4443 Sergeant KH (Kev) Foster. Centre Row: A22110 Flight Sergeant AT (Tom) Stoney, A32245 Sergeant HW (Dick) Bessell, 05879 Flying Officer LJF (Les) Reading, 022087 Flight Lieutenant LB (Leo) Brown, A22101 Warrant Officer LJF (Lyn) Heffernan, 033109 Flight Lieutenant RL (Smokey) Dawson, A5895 Sergeant ME (Blue) Colebrooke, A22221 Sergeant ED (Don) Armit, A22218 Sergeant FT (Fred) Collins, Flight Sergeant RLR (Reg) Lamb (RAF), Flight Lieutenant F (Frank) Easley (RAF), 033097 Flight Lieutenant LL (Scotty) Cadan, A33287 Sergeant C (Cec) Sly. Front Row: Flight Lieutenant J (Joe) Blyth (RAF), 04398 Squadron Leader DAS (David) Morgan (medical officer), Flight Lieutenant MS (Max) Scannell (RAF), Mr Eric Greenwood (Gloster Aircraft Company), 021960 Wing Commander NM (Mick) Kater (medical officer), 033188 Flight Lieutenant CD (Des) Murphy, 0383 Squadron Leader RC (Dick) Cresswell (commanding officer), 022094 Flight Lieutenant VB (Vic) Cannon, 033201 Flying Officer G (Geoff) Thornton, Mr Jock Gibb (Rolls-Royce Company), 021998 Flying Officer RR (Father) Davidson (operations officer), 033072 Flight Lieutenant IA (Joe) Lyons (intelligence officer), A33301 Warrant Officer CRA (Ron) Howe.

The RAAF pilots were progressively converted to the Meteor, conducting instrument training in the CAC Wirraway and flying the two-seat T.7s under instruction before going solo in the F.8. Training flights also continued in the Mustang; on 17 April, Sergeant Roy Robson was lost when he crashed on a night formation cross-country exercise near Matsuyama. The squadron marked Anzac Day with a flypast of six Meteors over British Commonwealth Occupation Force Headquarters at Kure as the war raged on the peninsula and the 3rd Battalion, Royal Australian Regiment, fought the Battle of Kapyong.

Except for Cresswell and Murphy, the Meteor was the first jet for the squadron's pilots and, for many, their first multi-engine aircraft. This introduced a new aspect of flight training which involved flight on one engine – known as asymmetric flight. Flying with one engine not producing thrust called for new handling skills for maintaining directional control while adjusting to the decreased performance associated with a failed engine, albeit simulated.

The side-hinged canopy of the Meteor T.7. The trainer was not equipped with ejection seats. (Australian War Memorial)

Cresswell later spoke kindly of the Meteor and organised an ongoing conversion system for newly arrived pilots:

> It was a very easy aircraft to fly. We called it the 'Gentlemen's aircraft'. Having two engines didn't make any difference. Being a jet didn't make much difference to blokes with experience. Some of the early guys had a bit of trouble.
>
> I had to form what I called an Orientation Flight at Iwakuni, and that flight was generally commanded by a retiring pilot from the squadron, going south. And I said, 'Well, spend a fortnight there and teach some of these guys what goes on.'
>
> That helped a whole lot and meant that the blokes coming from Australia, with no Meteor experience, but had jet experience on Vampires, could get about up twenty hours in the Meteor before they went into operations.

The Meteor F.8 was fitted with an early model Martin-Baker ejection seat which used an explosive charge to project the pilot and seat clear of the aircraft. The pilot would then separate from the seat and manually deploy the parachute. One Martin-Baker seat fired of its own volition when a component failed, ejecting Sergeant Tom Stoney who subsequently watched the Meteor fly orbits around him as he floated to earth beneath his parachute.

The role of the Meteor was still to be decided when General Earle Partridge visited Iwakuni and flew an F.8 after a conversion flight on the T.7 with Squadron Leader Cresswell. General Partridge had served in both world wars and trained as a test pilot in 1936. Partridge found the Meteor to be slow and lacking manoeuvrability, notably at high altitude. He also found the opaque metal rear section of the Meteor's canopy limited the pilot's rear vision in the very area from which an attack could originate. Despite the criticisms, Partridge believed the Meteor could fill the air-superiority role, flying fighter sweeps and escort missions. These would take place in conjunction with USAF Sabres of the 4th FIW, believing that joint tactics could compensate for the Meteor's shortcomings.

Squadron Leader 'Dick' Cresswell straps into a Meteor. (Australian War Memorial)

A few weeks later, comparison trials were flown between a USAF F-86 Sabre and an F.8 over two days. The Meteor was flown by Flight Lieutenant Scannell (RAF) and the F-86 was flown by Flight Lieutenant Steve Daniel (RAF) who had flown with the USAF in Korea. Daniel had flown the Sabre against the Mi-G15 in combat and used this experience to simulate the tactics of the Russian fighter. Below 25,000 feet, the Meteor compared relatively well and even possessed a faster rate of climb, however, the aircraft's performance significantly decreased above this altitude. This potentially left the Meteor vulnerable to diving attacks by the MiG-15, following which the latter could depart at a greater speed to the safe haven of Manchuria.

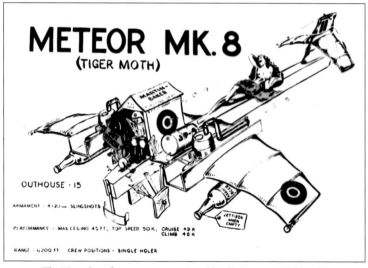

The Meteor's performance was not viewed kindly by some. (Ted Leach)

With the Meteor set for an air-superiority role, the squadron began to conduct flights to 30,000 feet where they fired the Meteor's four 20-mm cannons. Air-to-air cine gunnery commenced with cameras replacing live rounds as the Meteors fought mock dogfights. The firing of rockets from underwing rails also began and night flying was undertaken. In Cresswell's Commanding Officer's Report at the end of June 1951, he recorded, 'I can say confidently that the pilots are now ready to take these aircraft into combat.'

A Meteor T.7 trainer in formation with F.8s over Iwakuni. Note the difference in profiles. (Unknown via Dennis Newton)

In the squadron's absence from the Korean Peninsula, the ground war had stagnated to a geographical stalemate that would persevere until the war's end. Gone were the long advances north and south, replaced by localised offensives centred about the 38th Parallel, with the South Korean capital, Seoul, under UN control. This shift in war footing coincided with the beginning of peace negotiations between United Nations Command and the communist forces in Kaesong on 10 July 1951.

Progressively through July, the squadron moved the Meteors from Iwakuni to their new base at K14 Kimpo, near Seoul, as other pilots and ground crew were flown into K14 by the C-47s of No 30 Communication Unit. Despite episodes of poor weather, training continued in earnest. Guns were checked for firing at 35,000 feet to confirm there were no blockages, instrument flying was practised, and intercepts were flown against other aircraft. These were ground-controlled intercepts in which they were vectored to intercept other aircraft by a controller whose callsign was *Dentist*.

On 24 July, Lieutenant General Robertson sanctioned No 77 Squadron to resume operational duties in Korea. However, as not all aircraft had yet been fitted with an ADF, a minimum cloud base of 1,000 feet at K14 was required. With this lone proviso, the first operational sortie was scheduled for 29 July.

Led by Cresswell, the first sortie was a fighter sweep comprising 16 aircraft in two flights of eight at 30,000 feet and 33,000 feet. As Flying Officer Les Reading recalled in his April 2004 Australians at War Film Archive interview:

> The first mission was along what was called MiG Alley along the Yalu River which separated Korea from China and one hadn't done any air-to-air combat before and one wondered how it was all going to go when we mixed it up with the MiGs. There wasn't trepidation. There was wonderment I guess in a sense of expectation in wondering how it was all going to go.

> Well, we patrolled the Yalu at about 30,000 ft providing top cover for the Sabres for goodness' sake and on the first mission we watched the MiGs on the far side of the Yalu down at Antung take off and climb to get a fair sort of height advantage on us, they looked at us and then went back home.

Despite being uneventful, Squadron Leader Cresswell would note the squadron made RAAF history that day, '… by being the first squadron equipped with jet aircraft to enter into active operational duties.' Cresswell was not to know this was just the first of 15,000 operational sorties the RAAF Meteors would fly in the Korean War.

Some of the Mustangs used by No 77 Squadron were donated to the Republic of Korea Air Force by the Australian Government. (Australian War Memorial)

Gloster Meteor F.8

Gloster Meteor F.8 (Juanita Franzi)

TECHNICAL DATA

DESCRIPTION:
Single-seat interceptor and ground-attack fighter of all-metal, stressed-skin construction.

POWER PLANTS:
Two 16-kN (3,600-lb) thrust Rolls-Royce Derwent 8 turbojets.

DIMENSIONS:
Span 11.33 m (37 ft 2 in); length 13.59 m (44 ft 7 in); height 3.96 m (13 ft).

WEIGHTS:
Empty 4,853 kg (10,700 lb); normal loaded 7,121 kg (15,700 lb); max loaded 8,663 kg (19,100 lb).

ARMAMENT:
Four 20-mm cannon in nose; eight 27-kg (60-lb) rockets or two 454-kg (1,000-lb) bombs under wings.

PERFORMANCE:
Max speed 941 km/h (585 mph) at sea level; 869 km/h (540 mph) at 9,144 m (30,000 ft); cruising speed 666 km/h (414 mph); initial climb 2,134 m/min (7,000 ft/min); service ceiling 13,106 m (43,000 ft); range 1,234 km (767 miles) with ventral tank.

PILOT TRAINING IN THE JET AGE

The first pilots to see service during the Korean War were a mix of Second World War veterans and men serving with the British Commonwealth Occupation Force (BCOF) in Japan. As the war progressed, the demand for pilots increased and was exacerbated by the post-war reduction in personnel of the RAAF, with several pilots returning for a second operational tour.

RAAF and RAN trainees stand in front of their multi-engine trainer, an Airspeed Oxford. (via Owen Zupp)

Arriving in late 1951, a sergeant pilot would typically have undertaken a pilot's course on Tiger Moth biplanes, single-engine Wirraways, and ten hours on the Airspeed Oxford which had fixed pitch wooden propellers. Over the 12 months of training, they would have accrued around 200 hours of flight time, with 15 hours flown on instruments and 15 hours flown at night.

Pilots were introduced to the Mustang at No 3 Squadron, Canberra. (via Owen Zupp)

The next six months would see the pilot accrue 180 hours in fighter training on the Mustang with No 3 Squadron in Canberra before converting to their first jet, the de Havilland Vampire, at Williamtown, New South Wales. The jet-fighter element of training would take eight weeks and add a further 40 hours of flight time. Notably, the first flight in the Vampire was flown solo as the RAAF had yet to acquire any two-seat trainers.

The de Havilland DH.100 Vampire was used to train pilots in jet operations. A79-333 is seen here with a Mustang taxiing behind. Initially, only single-seat Vampires were available. (via Owen Zupp)

Having flown to Japan, the new No 77 Squadron pilot would have approximately 400 hours total flight time with 20 hours at night and 20 hours flown on instruments. Despite the Meteor being a twin-engine jet, they had still accrued a mere dozen or so multi-engine hours flown on the antiquated Oxford.

A Gloster Meteor T.7 two-seat trainer, parked within a revetment at Kimpo. (via Owen Zupp)

At Iwakuni, the pilot would undertake conversion onto the Meteor, first flying the two-seat T.7 with an instructor on two training sorties of an hour each before going solo in the single-seat F.8. Having flown four solo sorties, the new squadron pilot would be transferred to Korea. Having flown a further five solo familiarisation flights, including practice instrument approaches, the pilot would be deemed operational to fly missions with around ten hours of experience on the Meteor.

The Korean War would provide the catalyst for change in the future training of fighter pilots with the formation of No 2 Operational Training Unit at RAAF Williamtown in March 1952 to prepare fighter pilots for the demanding role. Additionally, the Fighter Combat Instructor course was established in 1954 to train specialist instructors in air combat.

Chapter 8
AIR-TO-AIR

It would take a few missions before the Meteors of No 77 Squadron would encounter their adversary, the MiG-15, for the first time. The hot, humid monsoon season settled over the Korean Peninsula and some missions were cancelled before they ever took flight. At times, aircraft were able to become airborne to practice ground-controlled approaches, but a number of fighter sweeps and bomber escorts did not occur.

When not flying, the pilots sought to improve their accommodation at Kimpo. The tents each accommodated four pilots and were reinforced with wood on the floors and midway up the walls, allowing the canvas to be rolled up for ventilation. As wood was a precious commodity, broken down crates were rebirthed as shelves and cupboards. In total, the squadron occupied 35 tents and six huts, the latter structures housing headquarters, a briefing room, and a crew room, with the remaining three assigned to the maintenance section and stores.

Aircrew accommodation at K14 Kimpo. (via Owen Zupp)

Kimpo was an extremely busy airfield with fighters and transport aircraft of all varieties using the sole 6,500-foot runway, which was covered in Pierced Steel Planking. Aircraft could be operating in the opposite direction on the single runway at peak times with the controller advising pilots to keep right to avoid traffic in the other direction. The squadron shared K14 with the United States Air Force's (USAF) 4th Fighter Interceptor Wing (FIW), flying F-86 Sabres, and the 67th Tactical Reconnaissance Wing, operating F-51 Mustangs, B-26 Invaders and RF-80 Shooting Stars.

K14 Kimpo as viewed across the engine cowling of a Meteor. (Unknown)

The Australians worked in close cooperation with the 4th FIW, both in the air and on the ground, sharing facilities and interacting on a social basis. The Americans were equally forthcoming in informally supporting the Australians with a variety of equipment, including flying suits and the like, just as they had been at the outbreak of the war when the Australians were operating Mustangs from Iwakuni. As No 77 Squadron had entered the jet age, the USAF had been pivotal in offering Dick Cresswell and Des Murphy exposure to jet operations and facilitated the use of a Sabre in trials against the Meteor. The concept of exchange pilots between the two nations was an aspect of the conflict that would last well beyond Korea and into the present day.

When the skies cleared, the fighter sweeps along the Yalu were without event. Surprisingly, when these sweeps were conducted in company with the Sabres, the Meteors flew at 30–35,000 feet, while the Sabres flew lower, between 20–25,000 feet. Operating well above their optimum fighting altitude, the Meteors were effectively flying top cover for the more-capable Sabres.

The escort missions were a different situation. These were predominantly flown in support of USAF B29 Superfortresses at lower altitudes between 20,000 and 25,000 feet, which suited the Meteor better. When the escorts were flown in conjunction with Sabres, the Meteors would fly close escort, while the Sabres flew a wider radius. On occasions, the Australians were also called upon to escort RF-80 Shooting Star reconnaissance aircraft which possessed very similar performance.

During this mix of missions, pilots encountered flak of varying degrees of accuracy but were never hit. Before any air combat occurred, Squadron Leader Dick Cresswell's tenure as Commanding Officer (CO) drew to a close; he was replaced by Wing Commander Gordon Steege, who, like his predecessor, was an officer of fighter pilot pedigree, having

Sabre FU-623

North American F-86E Sabre (Juanita Franzi)

'Pretty Mary and the Js' was the personal aircraft of Colonel Harrison Thyng, the commander of the 4th FIW from November 1951 until October 1952. He flew 114 missions and was credited with shooting down five MiG-15s.

TECHNICAL DATA

DESCRIPTION:
Single-seat fighter.

POWER PLANT:
One 26.69-kN (6,000-lb) thrust General Electric J47-GE-13 turbojet.

DIMENSIONS:
Span 11.31 m (37 ft 1 in); length 11.44 m (37 ft 6 in); height 4.30 m (14 ft 1 in).

WEIGHTS:
Operational empty 4,788 kg (10,555 lb); max loaded 7,455 kg (16,346 lb) with external tanks.

ARMAMENT:
Six 0.50-in machine guns.

PERFORMANCE:
Max speed 1,093 km/h (679 mph) at sea level, 967 km/h (601 mph) at 10,668 m (35,000 ft); max climb 3,072 m/min (10,080 ft/min); cruising speed 850 km/h (530 mph); service ceiling 14,387 m (47,200 ft); range 1,265 km (785 miles).

joined the Air Force before the outbreak of the Second World War. An ace in that conflict, Steege was credited with eight aerial victories, awarded the Distinguished Flying Cross, and commanded No 450 Squadron.

Wing Commander Gordon Steege (centre) and Squadron Leader Dick Wilson (far right) welcome senior American officers on a tour of K14 Kimpo. (Australian War Memorial)

Cresswell's role as CO of No 77 Squadron in the Korean War cannot be understated. He had come to the theatre with little advance warning following the combat loss of a respected and popular commander in Wing Commander Lou Spence. He had maintained the squadron at a high level of readiness and efficiency throughout its movement up and down the Korean Peninsula as the battle front fluctuated between offensives and counteroffensives. Flight and ground crews had operated in oppressive heat, monsoonal rains and below-freezing temperatures on snow-blanketed airfields. He had then overseen the complex transition of a ground-attack squadron operating single-engine Mustangs into the air force's first jet-fighter squadron flying operational fighter sweeps and bomber escorts. It was fitting that Cresswell became known as 'Mr Double Seven' in subsequent years.

MiG-15s began to be spotted regularly but generally did not engage the Meteors. They were seen taking off at Antung, others flew abeam the Australian aircraft but out of reach to the north of the Yalu, while some made a non-firing pass, diving at speed and accelerating away to the safety of Manchuria. On 18 August, the Australians even witnessed two MiGs flying barrel rolls as if in an impromptu exhibition. There was conjecture these early encounters were the MiGs, flown by Russians, scoping out the new adversary while intelligence was gathered on the Meteor. Regardless, on 29 August, the Meteors had their first duel with the MiG-15.

MiG-15 '823'

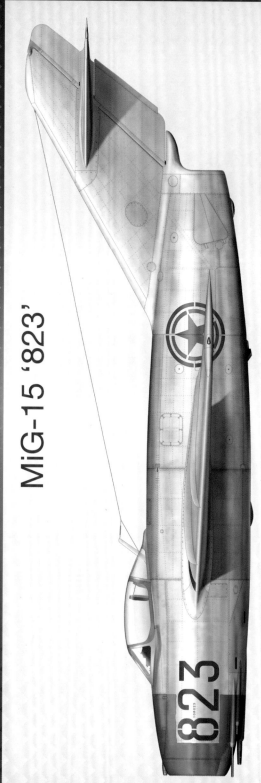

Mikoyan-Gurevich MiG-15 (Juanita Franzi)

Belonging to the 176th GIAP, 324th IAD, MiG-15 '823' was damaged on 12 April 1951 while attacking a USAF force bombing the Yalu bridges at Sinuiju. It was hit by fire from Colonel John Meyer of the 4th FIW flying an F-86A Sabre, but eventually returned to service. The nose number is often portrayed in blue; Russian sources record the numbers as black.

TECHNICAL DATA

DESCRIPTION:
Single-seat fighter

POWER PLANT:
One 26.5-kN (5,950-lb) thrust Klimov VK-1 centrifugal-flow turbojet.

DIMENSIONS:
Span 10.08 m (33 ft 1 in); length 10.10 m (33 ft 2 in); height 3.70 m (12 ft 2 in).

WEIGHTS:
Operational empty 3,681 kg (8,115 lb); gross 5,044 kg (11,120 lb); max loaded 6,106 kg (13,461 lb) with external tanks.

ARMAMENT:
Two 23-mm cannons and one 37-mm cannon.

PERFORMANCE:
Max speed 1,076 km/h (669 mph) at sea level, 1,107 km/h (688 mph) at 3,000 m (9,843 ft); max climb 3,072 m/min (10,080 ft/min); cruising speed 850 km/h (530 mph); service ceiling 15,500 m (50,900 ft); max ferry range 2,520 km (1,570 miles) with external tanks.

Eight Meteors, under the callsign *Anzac*, were operating in MiG Alley at 35,000 feet, divided into two flights of four. In company with 26 Sabres, the first flight, led by Squadron Leader Dick Wilson, spotted two MiGs below and dived to attack, but was soon under attack himself, taking hits to the port aileron and fuel tank. Wilson's pursuer was in turn attacked by two Meteors which sent the MiG diving away from the fight. At the same time, the second flight also came under attack from four MiGs. Number four in the formation, Warrant Officer Ron Guthrie, flying A77-721, was hit behind the cockpit; the aircraft began to shake violently. A second MiG destroyed the Meteor's tail, sending the aircraft out of control. At 35,000 feet, Guthrie ejected from his stricken fighter and came under fire from troops as he neared the ground beneath his parachute. He was taken prisoner and spent the duration of the war in brutal captivity.

Warrant Officer Ron Guthrie with ground crew and Meteor '721' from which he would be forced to eject on 29 August 1951. (Australian War Memorial)

By the end of August, the armistice negotiations had collapsed. At the squadron level, Steege's monthly report reflected his reservations regarding the Meteor's performance, writing that it was '… vastly inferior to the MiG' and '… outclassed in the fighter-v-fighter role.' He cited the disparity in maximum speed and that, in only fleeting contact, the MiGs had shot down one Meteor and damaged another without being damaged themselves.

Squadron Leader Dick Wilson and battle damage to Meteor A77-616 following the mission in which Ron Guthrie ejected from his doomed aircraft. (RAAF)

September 1 marked the signing of the Australia, New Zealand, United States Security Treaty, or ANZUS, as the Australians and the Americans were flying side-by-side in the skies over Korea. Days later on September 5, having escorted two photo-reconnaissance RF-80 Shooting Stars, eight Meteors were engaged by 12 MiG-15s. The MiGs initially passed in the opposite direction, 2,000 feet above the Meteors, before reversing direction and commencing attacks from the six o'clock position on the Meteors' tails. It was an organised and coordinated attack with a pair of MiGs making a firing pass and then pulling away before the next pair made their pass.

The Meteors had fired without success when Warrant Officer Bill Michelson was dealt a decisive blow that rolled the aircraft on its back and sent it into an out-of-control dive. With the tail severely damaged and the fuselage, aileron and flap holed, Michelson gently edged the aircraft out of the dive at 10,000 feet and limped home to Kimpo. In their post-combat narrative, the pilots noted the aircraft were painted with red noses. This would come to be recognised as aircraft of Russian squadrons.

On 6 September, Steege flew to Seoul with the squadron Intelligence Officer, Flight Lieutenant Ian Lyons, to meet with Colonel Myers, the Director of Operations at the USAF's Fifth Air Force Headquarters. At this meeting, the role of No 77 Squadron was adjusted with Steege recording that 'Meteors will not be included in the first line of fighter screen defence' and would not operate north of the Ch'ŏngch'ŏn River unless providing Combat Air Patrol (CAP) cover over fighter-bomber attack aircraft in that area. In addition to CAP, bomber escorts remained and the role of airfield defence was introduced. Under the new edict, the squadron was effectively removed from fighter sweeps in MiG Alley.

Meteors in formation over Korea. (Alan Royston)

This airfield-defence role involved the Meteors being scrambled to be vectored by the Dentist to intercept unidentified aircraft, which were nearly always friendly aircraft returning after action. To cater for this, two systems were implemented. 'Able Alert' required eight pilots in their cockpits from an hour before dawn to an hour after dawn. 'Baker Alert' required two pilots at five minutes readiness from 30 minutes before dawn to 30 minutes after sunset, with the crews changing over at meal times.

The changes were implemented against the backdrop of the United Nation's forces Operation *Strangle*, which sought to destroy railways, lines of supply and communications in an interdiction campaign. On an armed reconnaissance flying Meteor A77-15, Squadron Leader Wilson was hit by an explosive shell entering the cockpit; it severely wounded his right arm and hand, forcing him to fly to Kimpo with only the use of his left hand. He was treated in an American field hospital before being evacuated to Japan by a C-47 from No 30 Communication Unit and awarded an immediate Distinguished Flying Cross.

The pilots continued to see MiGs, at times up to 40, but no air combat ensued. Throughout September and October, the Meteors braced for a fight on several occasions, but nothing was forthcoming as the MiGs opted to engage the USAF Sabres in the battle for air superiority. One of the pilots in the Sabres was Squadron Leader Cresswell who was flying missions with the 4th FIW, where he claimed one MiG-15 damaged during his ten combat sorties.

September 26 was an exception to the rule when a bomber escort was changed to a fighter sweep in the Anju area after the aircraft were airborne. The 12 Meteors were attacked by 15 MiGs and, in the melee, Sergeant Don Armit's Meteor was hit, but remained flyable, while Flight Lieutenant 'Smoky' Dawson landed strikes upon one of the MiGs. Another MiG broke off the fight and turned south as his leader broke north towards the safety of the Yalu.

Sergeants Cedric Thomas and Vic Oborn gave chase; while the southbound MiG outran them, they doubted he would have sufficient fuel to make it back north after the pursuit.

Command of the British Commonwealth Forces in Korea changed on 5 October when Lieutenant General William Bridgeford replaced Lieutenant General Sir Horace Robertson, a fellow Australian. Later that month, 16 Meteors escorting B-29 bombers, and led by Squadron Leader Wilson, became entangled in an ongoing dogfight between MiGs and Sabres. During the fight, Flight Lieutenant Philip Hamilton-Foster's Meteor was badly damaged and, with one engine disabled, entered a spin. He was able to recover the aircraft and return to Kimpo on the one operational engine. Uninjured, he was mentioned in despatches for his efforts.

Wing Commander Gordon Steege post-mission. (Unknown via Dennis Newton)

The same day, the Meteors took part in the dramatic rescue of a pilot and observer of a Royal Australian Navy Fairey Firefly that had come down in a paddy field after taking heavy anti-aircraft fire during a ground-attack mission. The crew were surrounded by enemy troops, as successive pairs of Meteors flew CAP, strafing the area and providing cover until a helicopter from HMAS *Sydney* arrived to recover the downed airmen.

On 1 November, there was good news for the squadron. In recognition of its early entry into the conflict and the subsequent high level of performance, No 77 Squadron was awarded the Presidential Unit Citation by the President of the Republic of Korea, Syngman Rhee. It would be 1998 before the authority to wear the citation was finally granted.

Presidential Unit Citation

The President of the Republic of Korea takes profound pleasure in citing for

exceptionally meritorious service and heroism

No. 77 Squadron

for the award of

THE PRESIDENTIAL UNIT CITATION

This squadron entered the Korean war during the first week of North

Korean aggression. Flying Mustang aircraft it earned the highest reputation

for itself in giving close support to military operations for over eight

months of the campaign, and it won the admiration and friendship of all units

it supported.

It was then re-equipped with Meteor aircraft and has since continued its

fine record in the new roles allotted to it with these more modern aircraft.

Its performance throughout merits the highest praise.

While bestowed such an honour, the squadron found that bomber escorts of the B-29s had reduced significantly as the strategic bombing campaign was scaled back. Although the bomber escorts had subsided, fighter sweeps began to return in November and at times up to 60–70 MiG-15s could be seen in the air as they ventured well south of the Ch'ŏngch'ŏn River limit that had been imposed on No 77 Squadron operations. In clashes during the first days of the month, Royal Air Force (RAF) exchange pilot Flight Lieutenant Joe Blyth and Pilot Officer Ray Trebilco had encounters that resulted in vapour and smoke trailing respectively from MiGs, and Sergeant 'Bluey' Colebrook claimed a MiG damaged. Flying Officer Les Reading 'clobbered' one in its port wing root and left it streaming fuel; he would also be credited with a damaged MiG. Reading later described the engagement:

I had Wal Rivers as my wingman and we had just broken off from deterring 2 or 4 [MiGs] that were coming in, turned back and there were 2 coming in from our left side, our port side. I swung around and Wal tried to get onto the tail of one of them but it was going far too fast.

I swung around and he was going, it wasn't a matter of closing, he was going like that, terribly much faster than I was but I managed to get some deflection and shot him in the port, I think it was roughly in the port wingtip and he just streamed so much fuel it wasn't funny.

It filled the sky and a B-29 crew confirmed that that was destroyed. Both Wal and I saw one blow up but it couldn't be claimed as a kill because the cameras were freezing up at height and it had to be certain and confirmed.

Flying Officer Les Reading was credited with damaging a MiG-15 during an air-to-air engagement in early November 1951. (Defence via Les Reading)

The MiGs did not pose the only threat to the Meteors. On 11 November, the Meteors of Flying Officer Ken Blight and Sergeant Doug Robertson collided as they attempted to rejoin formation following a fighter sweep. Blight regained control of his aircraft after spinning twice and nursed his badly damaged Meteor close to Kimpo before ejecting. Sadly, his aircraft crashed into a field, killing a Korean on the ground. Robertson's Meteor flipped on its back on impact and spiralled down as pieces broke off through 18,000 feet. No parachute was seen and the squadron had lost its 17th pilot. This was the second mid-air collision with fatal results, the first occurring on 22 August when Flight Sergeant Reginald Lamb (RAF) and Sergeant Ronald Mitchell collided in the circuit area and crashed eight miles north of the runway at Kimpo; both men were killed.

As the weather turned ever colder, snow began to fall and puddles became slabs of ice. Covers were placed over the wings but attempts to use hydraulic fluid and kerosene as a form of anti-icing were unsuccessful. Brooms were used to sweep snow from the control surfaces and the Meteors would taxi out close behind another jet, hoping the warm efflux would keep their wings free of ice contamination. In the tents, a central pot-belly stove provided warmth and sweat-soaked flying suits were hung close by to avoid the moisture freezing. Steaks kindly offered by fellow American pilots could be left on tent flaps as a makeshift freezer until the meat could be cooked and devoured.

In the face of harsh conditions, the pilots began to accumulate serious mission tallies. Flying Officer Wal Rivers DFC had returned for a second tour and notched up 100 missions, as had Flight Lieutenant Joe Blyth (RAF), while Les Reading and Flight Lieutenant Geoff Thornton had each completed their 150th mission.

As November closed and December dawned, No 77 Squadron was to encounter a day that would change the course of their war and enter the annals of Air Force history. The menace of the MiG-15 was to take on a new scale.

Chapter 9
THE MIG MENACE

Since its first appearance over the Korean Peninsula, the MiG-15 had changed the balance of air superiority. Available in vast numbers, the MiGs had successfully ventured south of the Yalu River from their safe northern sanctuary where United Nations (UN) aircraft could not follow. The MiG-15 outperformed every straight-wing fighter in the theatre and the F-86 Sabre was its only true adversary in the skies.

No 77 Squadron's resident cartoonist, Flight Sergeant Bill Middlemiss, had this perspective on the MiG threat. Note the Soviet pilots depicted in the cockpits. (via Susan Middlemiss)

The presence of Russian pilots, or 'Honchos', had been identified, by the American pilots that encountered them, by their high skill level compared to their Chinese and North Korean colleagues. The Russians were experienced, with many of them Second World War veterans, when the 64th Fighter Aviation Corps deployed to Manchuria to command Soviet fighter regiments in early 1951. This injection of Russian pilots had set the stage for the famous air battles of MiG Alley.

In contrast, the MiGs had been reserved in their initial meetings with the Meteors, standing off at a distance while intelligence was gathered on the type. Gradually, the encounters became more active and air engagements took place but were limited in their scale, although the Meteor had fared badly by comparison. As a consequence, Wing Commander Steege had limited the operations of No 77 Squadron to south of the Ch'ŏngch'ŏn River to remove the threat of MiG Alley. However, by December, MiG Alley had expanded southward to no longer exclude the Meteor and fighter sweeps routinely saw and engaged MiGs. Even so, the engagements of November were balanced with both sides claiming damaged aircraft but with no apparent losses for the month.

A formation of Meteors peel away over rugged Korean terrain. (Australian War Memorial)

Unknown to the Australians, they had attracted the attention of Major General Georgi Lobov, commander of the 303rd Fighter Aviation Regiment. At the time, the UN had four jet-fighter squadrons employed exclusively as fighters, rather than ground attack. The 4th Fighter Interceptor Wing of the United States Air Force (USAF) had three squadrons flying F-86 Sabres, while the lone Commonwealth squadron operating in the role was No 77 Squadron with its Meteors. General Lobov would later claim he was the architect of the plan to destroy 77 Squadron and his motivation was not operational, but political. The USAF was present in high numbers but if the lone (at the time, as the South Africans did not receive Sabres until 1953) Commonwealth jet-fighter squadron could be devastated, the political ramifications may extend beyond Australia to Britain and potentially the United States.

The morning of 1 December was a fine, mild day in comparison to what the Korean Peninsula could provide in winter. That morning the squadron was briefed to conduct a fighter sweep in the Sunch'ŏn region, not far from P'yŏngyang. Three flights of four aircraft would operate under the callsigns of *Anzac* – Able, Baker and Charlie – with each Meteor carrying a full load of 20-mm ammunition. Flying Officer Geoff Thornton would lead the mission with Flight Lieutenants Max Scannell (RAF) and 'Scotty' Cadan the other flight leaders. Flight Lieutenant John 'Butch' Hannan and Sergeant Bob Strawbridge would remain south of P'yŏngyang as an airborne relay under the callsign *Stovepipe Dog*.

Across the Yalu River, 24 pilots of the Soviet 176th Guards Fighter Aviation Division were briefed that 16 pilots were to specifically target the Meteors while the remaining eight would fly top cover to guard against any subsequent attack by USAF Sabres.

The MiGs, led by Colonel V. Sergei Vishnyakov, were waiting at 30,000 feet when the Meteors arrived, flying much lower at 19,000 feet. The Russians pounced at speed with the advantage of height and surprise, attacking the rear of the Meteor formation. Sergeants Don Armit and Vance Drummond of Baker Flight came under immediate attack. Drummond was seen in a tight turn to starboard, streaming fuel as he called that his fuel tanks were hit and that he had lost his electrics. Another MiG pair pursued Flying Officer Wal Rivers and Sergeant Bruce Gillan in what was becoming a frantic battle as Thornton and his number three, Flying Officer Bruce Gogerly, made the break as MiGs fired at the lead flight.

Sergeant Vance Drummond was shot down and taken prisoner on 1 December 1951. (Australian War Memorial)

The sky was filled with twisting, turning aircraft seeking to gain an advantage. Gogerly was able to pull inside a MiG and deliver a burst of 20-mm cannon fire, seeing strikes to the wing root and fuselage, with fuel beginning to stream from the Soviet fighter. Elsewhere, a Meteor was seen descending in flames; Flight Sergeant Bill Middlemiss had been hit, flicked and rolled, recovering at an estimated 12,000 feet without an airspeed indicator, Machmeter or altimeter, and a holed port engine nacelle. During his descent, he had seen a burning aircraft in pieces falling to the ground. Scotty Cadan had been pursued by several MiGs and sent his Meteor diving earthward at its maximum speed with the enemy continuing to fire until they broke off at 7,000 feet. Cadan had seen two fires on the ground. The swirling maelstrom lasted for ten minutes and subsided with the suddenness of its onset. As the aircraft rejoined and reported in on their radio check, it was apparent there were aircraft missing. *Dentist* advised he had tracked Sergeant Bruce Thomson to within 80 miles of Kimpo and that Thomson had called for a heading to return but had never replied.

Returning to K14, the Meteors encountered an intense, accurate barrage of anti-aircraft fire only minutes after the air battle but did not lose another aircraft. When they landed at Kimpo, Flight Sergeant Don Armit and Sergeants Vance Drummond and Bruce Thomson had not returned. The only positive note was that Bruce Gogerly had claimed the squadron's first known MiG kill of the war at that time. Claims made in aerial combat can at times be difficult to positively confirm, given the speed and manoeuvring of those involved. The passage of time and access to Soviet records would later give credit for the first RAAF air-to-air victory of the war to Les Reading for his encounter in November.

That afternoon, two flights of four Meteors conducted a search, six of the pilots having flown in the battle. Steege, who had not routinely flown on operations, flew as number two to the leader, Squadron Leader Cedric Thomas. However, the search proved fruitless.

Battle damage to the tailpipe of a Meteor's Derwent engine. (Frank Field)

The impact of the losses was immediate. In recent weeks, four pilots and six aircraft had been lost, seriously affecting the squadron's operational capacity. Even more so, the decisive blow by the MiGs had summarily removed the Meteor from the fighter-sweep role and relegated the squadron solely to an air-defence role, operating out of both K14 Kimpo and K13 Suwon. Flying Able and Baker Alerts, the pilots would be scrambled to intercept unidentified aircraft relayed by the ground-controlled intercepts controller. The aircraft would usually prove to be friendly and the Meteors would return without incident.

Waiting in unlined tents to be called to fly in the midst of winter or strapped into the icy cockpit awaiting yet another fruitless scramble, seemed to be the only activities for the pilots. The airfield-defence role led to a negative effect on morale, despite Steege addressing the squadron and attempting to convince the pilots of its importance.

Some good news was forthcoming with prisoner of war lists having been exchanged on 18 December. It confirmed Gordon Harvey, Ron Guthrie, Vance Drummond and Bruce Thomson had survived their various misfortunes and were alive, albeit prisoners of the communist forces.

Flight Lieutenants Reading, Cannon and Scannell, Pilot Officer Trebilco, and Sergeant Colebrook all departed the squadron in December with more than 100 missions under their belts, 165 in the case of Les Reading and 169 for Trebilco. The month also saw Second World War veterans Flight Lieutenant Bill Bennett DFC and Flight Lieutenant Ian Purssey join the squadron with Flight Lieutenant Ray Taylor. However, a more substantial change in personnel was announced with a new Commanding Officer (CO) taking over the reins later in the month. This was Squadron Leader RT 'Ron' Susans DFC.

In an already distinguished Royal Australian Air Force career, Susans had flown Curtiss P-40 Kittyhawks over North Africa, Malta, Sicily and Italy with No 3 Squadron. In addition to leading bombing and low-level attacks, he was credited with shooting down two enemy aircraft, was mentioned in despatches and awarded the Distinguished Flying Cross. Later in the war, he flew Spitfires in the South-West Pacific as the CO of No 79 Squadron. Most recently, and significantly, earlier in 1951, Susans had attended the Day Fighter Leaders Course with the Royal Air Force at West Raynham, England. He had flown the Meteor extensively, including using it as a rocket platform.

Susans arrived on 20 December, assuming command a week later. He found squadron morale at a low ebb and was keen to see his new unit actively involved in the war again. On Christmas Eve, Susans led a four-aircraft scramble and signalled his intention to fly operationally as Wing Commander Lou Spence and Squadron Leader Dick Cresswell had done in their time leading No 77 Squadron.

Susans was aware the Meteor would not see action again as an interceptor against the MiG-15, but he also knew the Meteor had other redeeming qualities. It was rugged and could sustain a high degree of damage and still make it home. It was straightforward to maintain and its two engines offered a level of redundancy not shared by single-engine fighters. As Susans saw the situation, the Meteor was well suited to the ground-attack role, an argument its manufacturer had been making for some time.

Wing Commander Ronald Susans (right) took command of No 77 Squadron in December 1951 and moved quickly to change the unit's role to ground attack. (Australian War Memorial)

Without delay, he sought an interview with the commander of the USAF's Fifth Air Force, General Frank Everest. On meeting Everest, Susans proposed the use of the Meteor in a ground-attack role, citing it as the best rocket-firing platform in the theatre. He further emphasised that the pilots of No 77 Squadron were '… itching to try it out in this role'. General Everest was supportive of the proposal but stated that in doing so it was to utilise any capacity available beyond the airfield-defence role and that targets would be nominated by Fifth Air Force operations personnel. Susans was pleased with the opportunity to bring the Meteor back into the fray and advised Everest the squadron's target was to fly 1,000 sorties each month.

Next, the new CO set about organising nightly lectures on firing rockets and ground strafing, a task he delegated to 'Butch' Hannan. Sixty-pound (27-kilogram) rocket heads were flown in from Iwakuni and rocket rails fitted beneath the wings of the Meteors. Susans also initiated the withdrawal of his pilots from their daily-alert duties at K-13 Suwon. Within days, he had reinvigorated the squadron. It had established its reputation earlier in the war flying low-level close-support and armed-reconnaissance missions.

Major General Georgi Lobov had planned to destroy No 77 Squadron with the MiG ambush on 1 December but, within a month, the Australians were under new leadership and tasked with a new purpose – ground attack.

AIR VICE-MARSHAL RON SUSANS CBE DSO DFC DFC (US) AM (US)

One of the pivotal moments in the conduct of RAAF operations during the Korean War was the commencement of ground-attack operations for No 77 Squadron. The officer responsible for initiating the change and further enhancing the squadron's fine reputation was Wing Commander, later Air Vice-Marshal, Ronald Thomas 'Ron' Susans CBE DSO DFC DFC (US) AM (US).

Ron Susans surveys a map of the Korean Peninsula. (Martin Susans)

Before the Second World War, Susans served in the Citizen Military Forces and joined the Royal Australian Air Force (RAAF) at the outbreak of the war.

Following his completion of pilot training, Susans became a flight instructor at Point Cook before training as a fighter pilot in 1942. Late that year, he departed for the Middle East where he flew P-40 Kittyhawks with No 3 Squadron on operations over North Africa, Malta, Sicily and Italy. Throughout 1943, Susans flew a range of low-level ground-attack sorties against both land-based targets and shipping. Credited with two aerial victories and damaging several other aircraft, he was awarded the Distinguished Flying Cross in 1944.

Susans was posted to the war in the Pacific in 1944, flying Supermarine Spitfires with No 79 Squadron and becoming the unit's commanding officer in 1945. He subsequently led the squadron to Morotai until the war's end in 1945.

In 1946, Susans trained on the P-51 Mustang and commanded No 77 Squadron, British Commonwealth Occupation Force, the following year, returning to Australia in 1948.

He subsequently served in various roles and, notably, in 1951, undertook the Day Fighter Leader's Course in Britain, flying the Meteor F.8. It was this training that postured Susans as the candidate to take command of No 77 Squadron in December 1951.

Wing Commander Ronald Susans in the cockpit of his Meteor. The 'Mart & Geoff' nose art was dedicated to his two sons. (Australian War Memorial)

With the squadron relegated to the air-defence role, Susans immediately moved to enhance the unit's contribution to the UN effort, transforming it into an operational ground-attack unit within weeks. This became the squadron's primary role for the remainder of the war and one for which it earned a high reputation. Wing Commander Ron Susans led more than 100 missions and, on his departure, was awarded the Distinguished Service Order, having been previously awarded both the United States Distinguished Flying Cross and Air Medal.

Ron Susans (centre) briefs two of his pilots prior to a mission over North Korea. (Australian War Memorial)

Awarded the CBE in 1971, Susans held several significant postings until his retirement as an Air Vice-Marshal in 1975, including a senior role in the acquisition of the Dassault Mirage III for the RAAF. His son Martin also served in the RAAF, appropriately as a fighter pilot.

Chapter 10
SWIFT TO DESTROY

'Swift to Destroy'. The squadron badge would ultimately adopt the image of a Korean 'temple lion'.
It is affectionately known as the 'Grumpy Monkey'.

The new year was welcomed by a visit from 'Bedcheck Charlie' at 3 am. The obsolete Polikarpov Po-2 biplanes had overflown Kimpo in the darkness, their wood and fabric frames all but invisible to radar. Once overhead, they had released small bombs as anti-aircraft fire scythed the night sky. Neither the bombs nor the ground fire hit their mark but 'Bedcheck Charlie' had once again harassed the sleep patterns of the pilots and ground crews based at K14 Kimpo. A new makeshift ice rink, constructed from a large frozen mass, had also escaped unscathed.

The new year also saw the emergence of a major obstacle to peace negotiations that would continue to plague the possibility of an armistice in the months ahead. The two sides were in disagreement on the issue of prisoner repatriation with the Communists opposed to voluntary repatriation, returning only those prisoners that wished to return to their respective homelands.

For No 77 Squadron, the first mission of 1952 was flown by the Alert pilots out of K13 at Suwon. Once again, it was a ground-controlled intercept of friendly aircraft in the form of a single C-47 and nine F4U Corsairs. Multiple contrails were sighted high above, but the four Meteors returned to Suwon and, within a week, the air-defence missions would be solely based out of K14.

The ice rink at Kimpo provided a source of amusement for the members of No 77 Squadron. (via Susan Middlemiss)

Ron Susans officially gathered the squadron together on 4 January and briefed them on their new role as a ground-attack unit. The speed with which he had both given the squadron a new purpose, organising both men and machines in readiness, was in keeping with the squadron's motto 'Swift to Destroy'. Three days later, the first mission was scrubbed due to weather but, on 8 January, the Meteors were ready. Journalists had visited Kimpo in the morning and were introduced to the pilots before four of their number readied for the first mission in their new role.

As promised by General Everest, commander of the United States Air Force's (USAF) Fifth Air Force, the target had been selected by his operations personnel and passed onto the Australians in the form of a 'frag order', as it was known. The target was a water tower to the north-west of Kimpo and the mission would be led by the newly promoted Wing Commander Susans, with Flight Lieutenants John Hannan and Philip Hamilton-Foster, and Flying Officer Richard Wittman.

Typically, the briefing covered the key points of the mission regarding the weather, the target, radio frequencies and the route and formation to be flown. Additionally, any anticipated ground fire and emergency diversion plans would be briefed, along with any areas for safe ejection, although these were not always available for strikes on North Korea. The formation would operate under the new callsign of *Godfrey* with each aircraft carrying a full load of 20-mm ammunition and eight 3-inch 60-lb High-Velocity Aircraft Rockets.

With four aircraft flying the mission, the second pair stayed on the runway until they were beyond the point where the first two Meteors had taken to the sky and climbed away, 'cleaning up' their landing gear and flaps as they went. Soon the four aircraft joined up in a 'finger four battle formation' with the lead pair sitting 200 yards from the others. With their engines spinning at 14,000 rpm, the Meteors rocketed into the sky as Susans checked in with the ground controller, *Shirley*, and was cleared to the target.

Stores of 60-lb HVAR rockets as carried by the Meteor. (via Owen Zupp)

In conducting a rocket attack, the Meteors descended to 5,000 feet with the four aircraft slipping, one behind the other, into a line-astern formation. The leader rolled into a 20-degree dive and the other Meteors followed close behind, although varying their direction to avoid the anti-aircraft guns that may be tracking them. The dive angle had to be held steady for 10 to 20 seconds to allow the gunsight computer to assess the correct graticule position. Then, at 800 feet, the rockets were fired in salvos of four.

Godfrey One's rockets tore from their rails towards the target, trailing efflux. Within seconds, Godfrey Two freed his rockets and the pair behind did the same. The lethal ordnance sped away from the Meteors as if the jets were standing still and, within moments, the rockets were erupting in flames. As the air filled with smoke and rocket fragments, the Meteor pilots pulled their jets into a climbing turn with their throttles advanced to full power. The pilots fought the G-forces that drained the oxygenated blood away from their brains and towards their feet. They tensed their guts and strained their necks as they looked toward an escape path. Blacking out was a real threat and both man and machine groaned under the pull of gravity as vapour trails formed and streamed from the wingtips of the Meteors.

The rockets had scored six to seven direct hits with the tower left leaning away from the vertical and smouldering at the base. With their rockets expended, the four Meteors strafed the tower and a building nearby from which one of two automatic weapons was being fired on a tripod. Clear of the target and at a safe altitude, Susans called for each member of Godfrey Flight to check in on the radio. It was the standard means of taking a 'head count' that took place after every mission. As they set course for Kimpo, they strafed targets of opportunity and received ground fire passing Haeju. While the first rocket mission was completed without loss, the Meteors of Hannan and Wittman had received hits from ground fire. As the squadron was to learn, intense ground fire was to be the constant enemy of the new role. Exacerbating the danger, the Meteor's belly mounted ventral tank was vulnerable to fire coming from the ground and highly flammable.

Sergeant Phil Zupp inspects ground-fire damage to his Meteor's ventral tank following a mission. (via Owen Zupp)

On occasions, the rockets did not perform as planned as Sergeant Col King related during his May 2004 Australians at War Film Archive sitting:

> I had rockets hung up on one wing, and that helps to disturb the airflow a little bit. And the airflow was straight down the runway because the wind was straight down the runway. And whether the aircraft ahead of me applied power I don't know. But at least there were three aircraft ahead of me and the airflow was thoroughly chopped up.
>
> I was back to … the sort of speed you get back to on final approach. I think at that stage around 140. Suddenly one wing went down and the aircraft slipped and I took a little while to get control of it. I was very close to the ground when I finally got control of the thing again. I applied power and went around, came back and landed.
>
> Then I had to sit clear of the runway, pointing in a particular direction and waiting for armourers to come and disarm the rockets that were still hanging up.

Susans's leadership was evident in leading the first five armed-reconnaissance missions and rocket attacks before delegating such efforts to senior pilots such as Rivers, Hannan, Bennett and Browne-Gaylord. Even so, Susans flew the lead role on more rocket attacks than any other pilot through January, on occasions flying more than once a day.

Morale was high and the pilots were keen to participate in the ground-attack missions but, with low-altitude operations, losses were inevitable. Increasingly, aircraft were returning with damage from small-arms fire, flak and even debris thrown up from explosions created by an aircraft ahead. Flight Lieutenant Val Turner was injured and hospitalised when he crashed on approach to land on 24 January, after his Meteor developed engine problems when returning from an Airborne Alert mission. The crashed Meteor, A77-741, was salvaged from the field but written off due to damage.

Viewed from below, the Meteor's rocket load and vulnerable ventral fuel tank are prominent features in this image. (via Owen Zupp)

January 27 saw the squadron lose two pilots on the same day flying armed-reconnaissances in the Haeju area. It was late in the afternoon and the weather was poor with a low cloud base, limited visibility and snow falling in the area.

Having strafed buildings and vehicles and come under fire from the ground, Flight Lieutenant MAHA 'Harry' Browne-Gaylord DFC called that he had lost his altimeter and airspeed indicator. After a brief radio exchange with Flight Lieutenant Bill Bennett DFC, no further transmissions were heard from Browne-Gaylord.

A short time later, Sergeant Bruce Gillan was one of a pair of Meteors attacking a tower at Chwiya-Ri in difficult conditions of low cloud and snow. Having made his pass, Gillan pulled up but reported he had a hole in the starboard wing and was heading for home. Sergeant Al Avery, in the other Meteor, saw Gillan's Meteor streaming fuel and smoke and begin a gradual descent. Parts were seen coming from the cockpit section and, when Avery pulled alongside at only 200 feet above the ground, the canopy and ejection seat were missing. After Gillan's first transmission, there had been no further response to Avery's radio calls, and he had not seen a parachute.

Multiple searches were flown until darkness fell; they continued the next morning. No trace of Browne-Gaylord or his aircraft was found. Gillan's Meteor was located at rest on a mud flat in Haeju Harbour but there was no sign of life.

By month's end, the squadron had gone a long way to meeting the commitment Susans had made to General Everest. The Meteors had continued to fly scrambles and Airborne Alert missions along the line between Haeju and Singye from sunrise to sunset, in addition to the ground-attack missions. Two scrambles each day saw the Meteors meeting the withdrawing F-86 Sabres.

Although the squadron had not flown the 1,000 missions that had been proposed, it should be remembered the ground-attack role only commenced after the first week of January. Even so, the Meteors flew 965 hours across 781 missions, of which 140 were ground-attack missions. For a single month, this was the greatest number of hours and missions flown since the squadron had introduced the Meteor and the highest number of individual sorties flown since the unit entered the war in 1950.

It was an impressive record for the first month in a new role, but it had come at a significant cost. The squadron had lost three aircraft and, significantly, two pilots were posted as 'Missing – Particulars Unknown'. There would be more in the months ahead.

'BEDCHECK CHARLIE'

The Korean Air War is best known as the first jet war which saw aerial dogfights in 'MiG Alley'. However, in this new age of swept wings and supersonic flight, there was still a place for wood and fabric biplanes with a cruising speed of 60 knots (111 km/h). In the night skies over Korea, 'Bedcheck Charlie' had no need for speed.

It was a role of harassment, flying night missions to disturb the sleep patterns of those below. This was achieved by dropping fragmentation bombs and grenades, interrupting the sleep of pilots and ground crews. With a few exceptions, the raids caused minimal physical damage, although a No 77 Squadron Meteor was struck by shrapnel on one occasion.

The Soviet Polikarpov Po-2 was a wood and fabric biplane used to fly the 'Bedcheck Charlie' sorties. (Unknown)

While various aircraft were used, the Polikarpov Po-2 'Mule' was the most prolific. The design had first flown in 1927 and served through the Second World War in a range of roles, including night harassment sorties. These flights were flown by female Russian pilots who came to be known by the German troops below as the 'Night Witches' for the manner in which they silently glided down in their wooden craft, akin to witches upon their broomsticks. At the close of the war, the Russians began to phase out the ageing biplanes, exporting them to other communist nations. This included North Korea.

The Po-2 was a two-seat, open-cockpit biplane with a lone machine gun on a flexible mounting behind the rear cockpit. At the front, its five-cylinder engine was air-cooled with its exposed cylinders generating 125 horsepower (93 kW) to rotate its two-blade wooden propeller. The wood and fabric construction made the aircraft difficult to detect by radar, adding to their element of surprise.

The Korean War saw air power deployed through a multitude of means, from aircraft carriers to night fighters and strategic bombers to interceptors. In this diverse mix, the decades old Polikarpov Po-2 filled a specific niche as the night heckler known as 'Bedcheck Charlie'.

Chapter 11
FEBRUARY 1952

By February, the Korean winter was in full force with daily falls of snow and sleet hampering operations and presenting a difficult blank landscape by which to navigate. The change in role to ground attack had started strongly and the arrival of a further 2,000 rocket heads at the start of February signalled the intention to continue.

A snow-bound Meteor. (via Owen Zupp)

The nature of low-level operations exposed the Meteors to ground fire ranging from machine guns and flak to fire from gun pits, and intense small-arms fire. Mission after mission, aircraft returned with a range of holes through their airframes, some with the projectile still lodged in nacelles or nose cones.

Fundamentally, the Meteor was a rugged aircraft and able to continue flying having sustained damage; however, the ventral tank remained its Achilles' heel. The aircraft's two main fuel tanks were housed within the fuselage and only offered around an hour of safe airborne endurance operating at optimum power settings at 20,000 feet. Ground attack called for high power settings and flight at lower levels, both of which consumed more fuel. The 175-gallon (796-litre) ventral tank provided an additional 30 minutes of flight time and was essential to strike targets in North Korea from their base at Kimpo. Patrols were typically an hour long, with ground-attack missions lasting 40 to 50 minutes. Even when empty, the vapour contained within the belly mounted tank was highly flammable and exposed to the defensive fire that rose from below.

Gun-camera footage from Sergeant Phil Zupp's 23 February sortie showing direct strikes on two locomotives. (via Owen Zupp)

The squadron's deputy commanding officer, Flight Lieutenant 'Butch' Hannan was the next to fall to the ventral tank's vulnerable location. Leading a section of four in the Sibyon-Ni area on 6 February, the Meteors commenced a strike on two .50-calibre gun pits. Immediately after the attack, smoke and flames were seen to erupt from Hannan's Meteor as he attempted to climb and turn for Kimpo. With the conflagration growing by the second, Hannan ejected safely and was seen to reach the rugged terrain below.

The two Meteors of Squadron Leader Ray Taylor and Sergeant Phillip Zupp were diverted to search for the downed pilot. With the white parachute all but invisible against the snow, Zupp made an extremely low pass and, in turning back, having seen something on the snow, received a burst of ground fire that shattered his canopy and wounded him in the face. Zupp would receive a US Presidential Citation for the Purple Heart – a first for an Australian – in recognition of his injuries but it would be decades before the award would come to light. Years later, in a 1990 interview with the author, he recalled being hit by the ground fire:

> There was a huge 'roar' when the canopy shattered. My oxygen mask had been wrenched away and my goggles had been blown crooked and one lens was missing. Still climbing, I could taste blood in my mouth and feel some stinging and throbbing in my cheek and jaw. In the heat of the moment, I thought, 'If I'm dying, I actually don't feel that bad.'

Sergeant Phil Zupp's shattered canopy after being struck by ground fire on 6 February. (via Owen Zupp)

Not so lucky, 'Butch' Hannan was taken prisoner. The squadron now had five pilots known to have been captured. He joined Gordon Harvey, whose Mustang was lost in January 1951, and Ron Guthrie, who had ejected from his Meteor the preceding August. Bruce Thomson and Vance Drummond had ejected and survived the MiG-15 ambush of 1 December 1951; however, Don Armit had been killed in the encounter, aged 25.

Two days after Hannan's loss, the squadron participated in its first mission that delivered napalm in the head of an underwing rocket. The first trials of delivering the jellied petroleum had been undertaken months before at RAAF Williamtown back in Australia. No 91 Wing's Armament Officer, Flight Lieutenant John Smith, was credited with the development of the projectile with the first mission of its deployment labelled *Flaming Onion*. The squadron had previously delivered napalm from Mustangs in large tanks that skidded across the terrain but were difficult to deliver accurately. The rockets offered a more precise means of delivery.

Operation *Flaming Onion* and its four Meteors was led by Wing Commander Susans, each aircraft carrying a full load of 20-mm ammunition and eight of the newly armed rockets, each containing five gallons (23 litres) of napalm and a phosphorous grenade. The target was buildings at Chaeryŏng and the United States Air Force sent an RF-80 Shooting Star to follow the Meteors to photograph the execution and record the results. Sixty per cent of the rockets struck their target and started numerous fires, although the material used in the target buildings was not overly flammable.

PHOTOGRAPHY BY: 67TH TAC. RECON. WING 5TH U.S. AIR FORCE

PILOT: W/C R.H. SUSANS NO. 77 (1F) SQUADRON ROYAL AUSTRALIAN AIR FORCE

Wing Commander Ron Susans making the RAAF's first operational use of napalm rockets, the 'Flaming Onion'. Susans led four Meteors in the attack which was photographed by a USAF Lockheed F-80. (Australian War Memorial)

Flying his 38th mission, Sergeant Dick Robinson fell victim to the vulnerability of the ventral tank on 16 February in the Sinmak area while attacking buildings. Pulling out at 200 feet, fuel was seen streaming from the ventral tank and a fellow pilot called for him to jettison it. Before this was done, flames poured from the aircraft and the tail was seen to separate before the Meteor plunged into the ground.

With experience, more lessons were being learned about the squadron's new role. Following Robinson's loss, Susans briefed all pilots to immediately jettison the ventral tank and climb when a hit was suspected. He also expressed a need for a lightweight, disposable tank that could be jettisoned before every attack, rather than the heavy semi-permanent ventral tank that was currently in existence, a tank that took more than an hour to fit and cost about as much as a new Holden car in 1952.

Additionally, pilots began noting areas of intense anti-aircraft fire and created their personal 'Flak Maps' beyond the details provided in the pre-flight briefing they would receive from the Intelligence Officer. The map would plot the ever-moving 'bomb line' and pinpoint known flak traps and areas of known ground fire. Weaving on approach to the target when strafing was also encouraged to make the Meteor difficult for gunners to acquire.

The tactics regarding rocket operations were also modified as, increasingly, aircraft were being hit by ricocheting debris during the attack. Rather than a 20-degree dive and a rocket release at 800 feet, Susans modified the release to 1,000–1,100 feet and a 25–30-degree dive. One element of the attack that could not be modified stemmed from the gyro gunsight.

On a rocket attack, the aircraft and gunsight needed to be held steady before releasing the rockets, making the Meteors easy to track by gunners on the ground.

In strafing, the element of surprise and speed were two of the Meteors' prime weapons, but these too brought about issues. At low level at 300 knots (556 km/h), the aircraft's ailerons were heavy; this made aiming difficult. Attempting to align the aircraft with the target using rudder inherently led to snaking, with the gunsight moving back and forth across the target. At 350 knots (648 km/h), it was impossible to achieve the aiming point using ailerons. Susans proposed the ailerons be modified.

Additionally, the Chinese were experts at using camouflage. They could conceal ammunition and fuel dumps beneath stacks of rice. Trucks could be parked in natural depressions and concealed. At other times, trucks could be used to draw the low-flying Meteors into flak traps, or into ravines across which cables had been stretched. As a consequence, the Meteors flew even lower, around 200 feet, to identify such targets, thus exposing them to ground fire, at times from gunners on ridges above them. The reality also existed that unless adequate altitude could be achieved before ejecting, the early generation of Martin-Baker ejection seat did not offer the pilots sufficient time to release from the seat and open a viable parachute canopy.

An aerial view taken rolling in for a strike upon a bridge. (Unknown)

Throughout the month, a range of targets was struck as the squadron played its role in the interdiction campaign of the Fifth Air Force. Warehouses, boats, railyards, trains, trucks and troops were some of the diverse targets assigned to No 77 Squadron. One mission alone destroyed 28 vehicles. All the while, the Meteors continued to fly combat air patrols and air-defence missions as Susans had agreed.

He had also set a goal of 1,000 missions a month and, on 27 February, the total stood at 907. With the assistance of fine weather and a 29-day month, the squadron recorded 1,007 missions for February. Along with praise for the pilots, Susans commended those on the ground that kept the aircraft flying. Despite a shortage of aircraft due to combat losses and ongoing damage from ground fire, the members of No 491 Maintenance Squadron continually provided more than 90 per cent of the aircraft serviceable and ready to fly at the commencement of each day's operations.

Furthermore, as the 1,000-mission target loomed, the supply of petrol, oil and lubricants ran out with 24 hours to go. Ground crews worked through the night and continued through the following final day, refuelling the Meteors manually from 44-gallon (200-litre) drums. Without their effort, the milestone would not have been achieved. Beyond the harsh weather and explosive qualities of some of the stores they handled, there was further risk in what they did; in the early hours of 9 February, K14 was the target of saboteurs. A firefight broke out and five of the perpetrators were killed.

February 1952 would be recorded in the squadron's history for many reasons. The record month had been achieved in 1,300 hours of flying, expending 80,000 rounds of 20-mm ammunition and 2,600 rockets, of which 32 carried napalm. A full-effort mission called for 16 aircraft; the squadron had 23 fully trained pilots, including Susans. A number of pilots had been decorated by both the Commonwealth and the United States.

The 1,000-mission month had come at a cost. Sergeant Dick Robinson had been lost and damage to the ventral tank had again been the culprit. In its role of ground attack, the squadron had proved able and effective and, as the war continued in stalemate, the demand to strike targets increased even further.

The official war artist in Korea, Ivor Hele, captured the return of Meteors from a sortie. (Australian War Memorial)

SERGEANT PHILLIP ZUPP

On 6 February 1952, Sergeant Phillip Zupp was patrolling near Sibyon-ni, Korea, in a Meteor F.8 of No 77 Squadron RAAF. Almost immediately, he was called to search for Flight Lieutenant 'Butch' Hannan who had been forced to eject after his aircraft was hit by ground fire. In a heavily defended area, Zupp made several low passes looking for his squadron-mate when he thought he had caught a glimpse of a pilot's red 'marker scarf' on the snow. He wheeled the Meteor around at tree-top height to investigate.

Sergeant Phillip Zupp seated in A77-446 'Black Murray' – the usual aircraft of his course mate, Sergeant Ken Murray.
(via Owen Zupp)

His next memory was the deafening roar as his cockpit seemingly exploded around him. With the canopy in pieces, the freezing airflow rushed by at 300 knots (556 km/h). He heaved back on the control column as his Meteor's ventral tank was now perilously close to the ground. Struggling to gain his orientation, he reached to straighten the askew oxygen mask and shattered goggles, his face now stinging from embedded Perspex and shrapnel (material that would ultimately be removed by surgery in 1990).

He was able to return the damaged Meteor to his base at Kimpo where he was treated for his wounds. Leaving the hospital later that day of his own volition, he was to fly two sorties the following morning.

His efforts impressed the American personnel and, unknown to him, Zupp was recommended for the US Purple Heart – a first for an Australian. Despite the award being recommended at all levels of military command and government, the right to wear the decoration was denied by a Commonwealth department in London. Knowledge of the award only surfaced in the 1990s when the US Presidential Citation and other documents came to light.

A close call. The shattered lens and deformed frame of Phillip Zupp's goggles, the result of being hit by ground fire on 6 February 1952. (via Owen Zupp)

Zupp's previous military service entailed training as a navigator in the Second World War before he changed Services and saw active service as an Army commando in New Guinea. At the conclusion of the war, he was among the first contingent of the British Commonwealth Occupation Force to sail for Japan, where he was stationed at Hiroshima. Ultimately, he returned to the Royal Australian Air Force and, after initially enlisting as an engineer, re-mustered for pilot training, before going on to fly 201 missions as a fighter pilot in Korea.

Phillip Zupp with a ground crew member. The 60-lb rockets are visible beneath the wing of the Meteor. (via Owen Zupp)

In a fortunate circumstance, Australia's Chief of the Defence Force, Air Chief Marshal Mark Binskin AC, became aware of the issue regarding the Purple Heart. He pursued the matter and learned the award could have been made in 1952 if it had not been blocked in London. Now, as he had passed away in 1991, it could not be presented personally. However, the United States Air Force still wished to recognise Zupp's actions on that day in 1952 and posthumously awarded him a second US Air Medal in 2018 to sit alongside his mentioned in despatches.

Sergeant Phillip Zupp AM (US)
A11439
No 77 Squadron RAAF
Korea 1951–52

Chapter 12
STRIKING THROUGH THE STALEMATE

Wind, snow and freezing temperatures continued to play a significant role in operations and seemed to mock the untimely arrival of cricket equipment at Kimpo. For the pilots on pre-dawn air-defence duties, sitting atop frozen water rations in their ejection seat, and without heating, the duty was not highly regarded. Even when airborne, the cockpit heating took a significant time to become effective and would not be of much benefit for the bulk of a mission.

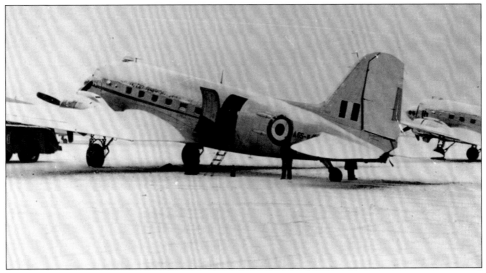

The harsh weather made all operations difficult, here a C-47 Dakota is shown with a coating of snow. (David Hitchins)

In the face of the poor weather, turbulence and terrain, the C-47s of the renamed No 30 Transport Unit continued to provide vital support to No 77 Squadron and the Australian Army. The first two months of the year had seen the unit fly 200 missions including medevacs, VIP transport, daily 'Army courier' flights, and freight transfers. The eight aircraft and seven crews had evacuated 900 patients to Japan and notched up one million miles flown over the preceding 16 months.

March saw the rocket strikes and losses continue. On 9 March, having made a first rocketing attack on revetments containing troop concentrations, Sergeant Ian Cranston pulled up from the second pass streaming fuel from his ventral tank. Seconds later, a fire developed before the aircraft rolled on its back and spun into the terrain. Late in the month, Sergeant Lionel Cowper failed to pull out of a dive during a rocket attack and crashed into the ground below. In such losses as Cowper's, it was difficult to identify the cause. The pilot may have been killed or incapacitated by ground fire or become so focused on the target that he was too slow to commence his pull up after the attack. There was also consideration given to the transition from the Mustang to the heavier, faster Meteor. The twin jet carried more inertia into the rocket attack so, until experience on the Meteor was gained, previous experience on the lighter Mustang in training may have played a role.

The loss of pilots saw new arrivals transition to the Meteor in Iwakuni before posting to Kimpo. Additionally, some pilots, such as Sergeants Max Colebrook and 'Scotty' Cadan, volunteered to return to Korea for a second tour. The attrition of aircraft was also significant with 18 Meteors lost by mid-March 1952 through accidents and combat losses. At this time, the second order of 22 Meteors began to arrive, once again having been ferried to Singapore before being shipped as deck freight to Japan.

Some positive news came periodically in the form of a 'Gong Night' when decorations were bestowed upon the recipients. American awards of the Distinguished Flying Cross (DFC), Air Medal and Oak Leaf clusters were presented by the commanding officer of the United States Air Force's (USAF) 4th Interceptor Fighter Wing that shared K14 with the Australians. In early 1952, that officer was Colonel Harrison Thyng, a Second World War fighter ace who subsequently became a jet ace in Korea, with five claims in each war.

Kimpo, South Korea. 1952. pilots of no. 77 Squadron RAAF assembled in the aircrew club after ceremony at which they were invested with the United States Air Medal By Colonel Harrison R. Thyng, commander of the USAF 4th fighter interceptor wing. They are: standing, left to right, Squadron Leader W.R. Bennett, DFC; Flying Officer Bruce Gogerly; Sergeant K. Murray; Col. Thyng; Wing Commander R.T. Susans, DFC; co no. 77 Squadron; Warrant Officer A. Philp and Sergeant R.V. Oborn. Kneeling are: left, Flight Sergeant A.J. Avery and right, Sergeant F. Blackwell.

Weeks after his arrival for a second tour, Max Colebrook went missing. On 13 April, after attacking a target, he climbed away and was advised that his ventral tank was on fire. Seconds later Colebrook called that he had jettisoned the ventral tank, both engines were operating normally and he was heading for home. Nothing further was seen or heard of the pilot and his Meteor.

A further loss came on 22 April when Squadron Leader Bill Bennett led an attack on buildings in the Chinnampo area. Intense ground fire struck his ventral tank and shot off the elevator trim control on his tailplane. Bennett jettisoned the ventral tank but his number two, Flight Lieutenant Ian 'Bill' Purssey, reported he had also been hit; Bennett could see that the other Meteor was on fire and called for Purssey to jettison the ventral tank. Bennett witnessed the wing of the Meteor separating as Purssey ejected above the Taedong River estuary, too low for the parachute to open.

The Meteor pilots had started to see MiGs again, although no engagements took place until 4 May when Pilot Officer John Surman brought down a Soviet fighter while on a patrol between Haeju and Singye with Sergeant Ken Murray in the lead. The Meteors were patrolling at 15,000 feet, an altitude more suited to the performance of the aircraft. Nine MiGs were sighted 2,000 feet above when two of their number dived on the Meteors. When Murray broke, Surman was initially separated by 600 yards and saw a MiG firing on his leader from behind. Surman dropped in behind the MiG and fired, closing from 200 yards to just 30 feet (roughly 180 metres to barely 10!) where he witnessed debris break away from the tail and fire pour from the side of the fuselage. He then broke away to avoid colliding with the enemy aircraft and did not sight it again. John Surman had been posted to the squadron a fortnight earlier and was a graduate of the first course from the RAAF College.

An artist's impression of a Meteor's victory over a MiG-15. (Artwork by Dennis Newton)

A new interdiction campaign had been underway since March, named Operation *Saturate*. Previous operations by the Fifth Air Force had seen North Korean forces repair damage quickly, despite a bombing campaign by day and night. Operation *Saturate* was aimed at the Main Supply Route (MSR) and creating significant damage to North Korean railway lines, thus requiring heavy equipment to repair the damage and consequently slowing any progress. USAF fighter-bombers were chosen for the attacks and, after a long absence from flying fighter sweeps, No 77 Squadron was assigned the task. Unlike the previous sweeps of 1951, where the Meteors flew top cover for F-86 Sabres, they would be operating below 20,000 feet.

On the first day of fighter sweeps, 8 May, the squadron flew 76 sorties as the USAF fighter-bombers struck the MSR in the largest strike since the war commenced. One Meteor pilot flying that day was another graduate of the first RAAF College course, Pilot Officer Bill Simmonds. Patrolling at 15,000 feet, the flight of four Meteors was south-west of P'yŏngyang when they were attacked from behind by two MiG-15s. Simmonds was flying in the number four position and described the engagement when recorded for the Australians at War Film Archive in May 2000:

> The first indication I had of any real danger was when I observed three distinct lines of tracer ammunition going over my left wing. Instinctively, I pulled away from these bullets and by simply just going into a hard right turn. I'd hardly begun the turn when I observed a MiG-15 fly straight underneath me.

> My immediate impression was that this was too good an opportunity to miss so I reversed and started to follow him and I accelerated at the same time. When he was probably a couple of hundred yards in front, I started firing.

> … although I was accelerating and he was still moving away from me but finally some of the bullets obviously hit his aircraft because there was a large plume of smoke … emitted from around the fuselage area and the next thing I saw was this aircraft sort of pitch up obviously out of control and as I was aware that there were other MiGs in the area, I rolled to the left into a hard turn just to ensure that there was nobody behind me.

> And as I went into the turn the flight leader observed the pilot of the MiG to bail out. He ejected and his parachute deployed and presumably he landed safely. Meanwhile we, our section of four aircraft, regrouped and we continued flying there for another ten or fifteen minutes before we re-deployed or flew back to the base. The whole thing took maybe thirty seconds but that's the nature of, you know, air combat these days.

Others in the formation had also witnessed the MiG initially climb before falling over on its back and into a spin. The leader, Flight Lieutenant Eric Ramsay, saw a parachute below and the MiG crash into the ground.

MiG Killers. Pilot Officers Bill Simmonds (left) and John Surman congratulate each other after downing MiG-15s on 8 May and 5 May 1952 respectively. Both were graduates of the first RAAF College intake. (Australian War Memorial)

Pilot Officer Donald Robertson, who had also recently arrived from the RAAF College, was the winner of both the Queen's Medal and the Sword of Honour on graduation. Mid-May, he was in one of four Meteors tasked to attack buildings to the east of Sariwon. In making the attack, he was seen to fire only four of his eight rockets at an unusually high altitude of 3,000 feet. The Meteor then veered sharply to the right and crashed, exploding on impact. The call of 'Two's down!' came from Sergeant John Myers who was behind Robertson at the time. The squadron recorded that it believed that Robertson was hit by ground fire during the dive to the target.

As May drew to a close, another 'Gong Night' saw officers and NCOs receiving American decorations, including American DFCs and Air Medals. Among the recipients was Wing Commander Ron Susans who received both the DFC and Air Medal and was notably awarded the Distinguished Service Order by the Commonwealth. He departed for Iwakuni the next day on his return trip to Australia.

Susans's contribution to the Australian presence in Korea was significant. He arrived at Kimpo in December 1951 and was confronted with a squadron low on morale and needing a challenge. Within days he had delivered No 77 Squadron a new purpose and begun organising their transition to the ground-attack role. He innovated the use of napalm on rockets and continually reviewed the tactics the squadron employed. Leading from the front, Susans flew more than 100 missions with the vast majority being strafing and rocket attacks.

Squadron Leader Bill Bennett DFC replaced Susans as the temporary commanding officer. Like his predecessor, Bennett was a veteran fighter pilot of the Second World War. He had flown Spitfires over Belgium, France and the Netherlands before transferring to an Australian squadron in mid-1944. As a flight commander, his Spitfire was shot down attacking a V2 rocket site with Bennett remaining a prisoner of war for the remainder of the war.

Kimpo, South Korea. 1952. squadron leader W.R. Bennett (right) deputy commanding officer of no. 77 squadron RAAF congratulates Flight Lieutenant W.B. Rivers, D.F.C., on completion of his 250th operational mission with no. 77 squadron.

By June, the weather was hot; mud had replaced snow at Kimpo. Personnel were issued with mosquito nets to guard against malaria. In the air, the war had also changed for No 77 Squadron. One constant was the leadership following Susans's departure. Bennett also believed in leading from the front and flew numerous strike and armed-reconnaissance missions.

On 9 June, Flight Lieutenant Pete Middleton led four Meteors on an armed reconnaissance that attacked several trucks. Pilot Officer John Surman, who had recently brought down a MiG-15, was flying as number four as the flight turned to make a second pass. As they attacked the vehicles, Surman's aircraft was seen to "mush" into the ground, burning on impact.

Airborne alerts had all but vanished by the first week, replaced by armed reconnaissance, strikes and fighter sweeps. Armed reconnaissance and strike missions differed, both in their composition and their objectives. The former comprised four or eight Meteors equipped with full loads of 20-mm ammunition and were assigned an area to observe and attack viable targets that were discovered. Strike missions were pre-briefed with a specific target assigned to between eight and 16 Meteors, the latter being termed a 'maximum-effort' strike. The aircraft carried a full load of 20-mm ammunition in addition to eight 60-lb (27-kg) rockets. Ultimately, some aircraft were fitted with double rocket rails, allowing the carriage of 16 rockets.

The peace negotiations at Panmunjom had broken down in May and General Mark W Clark had succeeded General Matthew Ridgeway as the head of the United Nations Command. Clark observed that the interdiction strategy had been thwarted in its overall effectiveness by the North Korean ability to rapidly repair road and rail lines and re-establish the MSR. He recognised that air power was the most effective method of exerting pressure on the Communists without excessive Allied loss of life on the ground. A strategy of attrition by targeting specific infrastructure was deemed to be 'air pressure'. The strategy commenced in late June with hydroelectric power plants as the first targets, rendering 90 per cent of North Korea's power generation infrastructure out of service and causing a near-total blackout across the country.

The increase in offensive operations extended beyond No 77 Squadron to the Fifth Air Force and the broader Far East Air Force. The strategy sought to use air pressure to achieve favourable peace negotiations. For the Meteor squadron, both the intensity and inevitable losses would continue.

BROTHERS IN ARMS

The Korean War witnessed a strengthening of ties between the Royal Australian Air Force (RAAF) and the United States Air Force (USAF), particularly the Fifth Air Force. However, the Royal Air Force (RAF) also contributed significantly to the RAAF, particularly as it moved into the jet age with the employment of the British-built Gloster Meteor F.8 and its training counterpart, the two-seat T.7.

Inspecting a bomb on an F-80 Shooting Star are, left to right, Flying Officer Ken Blight and Sergeant Ron Mitchell of No 77 Squadron and Lieutenants Holmes (standing) and Sellers of the USAF. (Australian War Memorial)

Before the introduction of the Meteor, No 77 Squadron's operation of the North American P-51 Mustang had benefited from a ready supply line of interchangeable expertise, components and ammunition with the USAF. A transition to the North American F-86 Sabre may have maintained some of these synergies but American production was struggling to supply the USAF with more than the two squadrons they had in Korea when the MiG-15 made its presence known in 1950.

Consequently, the Meteor brought with it the challenges of a new aircraft type that required pilots and ground crew to be trained and airframes to be supported. The RAF rose to meet these challenges with both the supply of instructors to convert the Mustang pilots to jet operations and subsequently provided a steady stream of exchange pilots throughout the war that would ultimately see 32 fly on combat operations. Five of these men became casualties of the Korean War.

The first four RAF pilots attached to No 77 Squadron were Flight Lieutenants Easley, Blyth and Scannell, and Flight Sergeant Lamb. Two were posted from Advanced Flying Schools where they were instructors, while the New Zealander Max Scannell was a highly respected pilot and winner of RAF aerobatic competitions. All four were highly experienced in flying the Meteor.

A group portrait of the first RAF pilots to serve with No 77 Squadron in Korea. Left to right: Flight Sergeant Reg Lamb and Flight Lieutenants Max Scannell, Joe Blyth and Frank Easley. Highly experienced Meteor pilots, they trained the RAAF pilots when Meteors arrived in Japan. (Australian War Memorial)

The first Meteors arrived on board HMS *Warrior* in late February. These aircraft had narrow engine intakes; Dick Cresswell sought to modify the Meteors to the larger intakes available to increase engine performance. The RAF were forthcoming with haste, flying the nacelles to Japan from the United Kingdom. All four of the RAF training team arrived in March and sought to fly operational missions in the Mustangs; they were granted permission by Cresswell to do so. The four pilots flew close-support and armed-reconnaissance missions in the Mustangs until these aircraft were withdrawn from operations in April to allow the squadron to convert to the Meteor.

On exchange from the RAF, New Zealander Flight Lieutenant Max Scannell (left) meets Australian Hollywood star Errol Flynn. (RAAF)

The conversion training involved numerous ground lectures on the aircraft's systems and jet operations. The knowledge base was also enhanced when Max Scannell flew a comparison trial in the Meteor against a USAF F-86 Sabre during May 1951. The Sabre was flown by Steve Daniel, an RAF pilot who had flown the type on exchange with the USAF. For the

Mustang pilots, conversion to the Meteor typically involved a pair of one-hour sorties in the two-seat T.7 before being sent solo in the single-seat F.8.

The RAF pilots were well versed in operating in poor weather and were highly trained in instrument flying when compared to the Australians. Cresswell noted the importance of this skill and incorporated instrument flying and ground-controlled approaches into the training. However, he recognised this was an area in which RAAF pilot training would need to improve and this shaped one aspect of his future approach to operational training.

A Meteor overflies an RAF Sunderland off the coast near Iwakuni, Japan. (Doug Norrie)

The RAF training team extended their stay with No 77 Squadron and flew operationally in Korea, with Scannell and Blyth both being involved in skirmishes with MiG-15s in the days flying fighter sweeps. Flight Sergeant Cruickshank was the first RAF pilot to lose his life when he was involved in a mid-air collision in the circuit area at Kimpo in August 1951. Flight Lieutenants Easley, Blyth and Scannell would return home later in the year with the latter two both having surpassed 100 missions.

There was undoubtedly interest from the RAF regarding the performance of the Meteor and the tactics that emerged from the first jet war. Additionally, the MiG-15 would be Britain's adversary over Europe should that Cold War thaw so intelligence on the Soviet fighter was of great value. This interest was highlighted in February 1952 when two representatives from the RAF Operational Technical Analysis branch visited the Australians and met with Wing Commander Susans to discuss the type of operations and aerial warfare in Korea. Their visit coincided with the arrival of further RAF exchange pilots of whom a constant rotation would exist until the Armistice in July 1953. A small number of RAF pilots also flew Dakotas with No 30 Transport Unit from Iwakuni, Japan.

Besides the five men killed, one of the RAF exchange pilots, Olaf Bergh, was taken prisoner. Another, Flight Lieutenant Michael Whitworth-Jones, was sadly killed a month after his return from Korea in 1953 when his de Havilland Venom broke up in flight. A number would attain air rank in the years that followed and one, Keith Williamson, would rise to become Air Marshal Sir Keith Williamson GCB AFC. The contribution of the RAF and its personnel was pivotal to the RAAF entering the new age of jet-fighter operations.

Chapter 13
AIR PRESSURE

At No 77 squadron, July 1952 was rung in with a Yellow Alert at midnight, warning of an 'unidentified aircraft in the vicinity of K14'. The alert did not escalate to Red Alert, which would have warned of an 'Attack by aircraft. Will bomb or strafe.' Fifteen minutes into the new month, the alert was cancelled. Weather precluded flying on the first day of July, but the squadron was inspected by senior officers of the United States Air Force's (USAF) Fifth Air Force, while war artist Major Ivor Hele arrived to capture the pilots, ground crews and aircraft at work at Kimpo.

Also arriving that month was Wing Commander Peter Ottewill GM (Royal Air Force) who, as a sergeant, had flown Hawker Hurricanes with the RAF in 1940 before being shot down over Dieppe and badly burned. His role in Korea was related to his current posting as the Commanding Officer of No 2 Operational Training Unit at RAAF Williamtown. Over three weeks, Ottewill observed the fighter squadron in action and flew actively on both armed reconnaissance missions and fighter sweeps, gathering information that could be employed in future fighter pilot training.

A preceding Meteor can be seen rolling in on a target below. (Ted Jones)

Trucks were a primary target of the armed-reconnaissance missions; however, some attacks were withheld as the trucks were positioned in areas of known flak traps. On 8 July, Sergeant Ken Smith led four Meteors that found and then strafed two trucks in a ravine. Smith was seen to pull out of the dive but did not clear a nearby hillside, exploding in a sheet of flame. He was posted as 'Missing – Believed Killed in Action'. In the coming days, the Wing Adjusting Officer arrived again, this time to arrange Smith's affairs and personal belongings. The attrition of pilots and aircraft was substantial; six RAF pilots arrived to ease the burden. Of these six, three were destined to be shot down.

Squadron Leader Bennett's temporary command of No 77 Squadron was completed with the arrival of Wing Commander Jack Kinninmont DFC and Bar. Kinninmont had joined the Royal Australian Air Force (RAAF) before the Second World War and claimed two aerial victories over the Japanese, while flying the inferior Brewster Buffalo, before the fall of Singapore in February 1942. Later in the war, Kinninmont flew with fighter squadrons in New Guinea and was awarded a Distinguished Flying Cross in 1944 and a Bar to the decoration in 1945. Just as Susans had done, Kinninmont made an immediate trip to Fifth Air Force Headquarters and, only days later, flew operationally, leading 12 Meteors on a strike mission.

Away from combat, the squadron had adopted the Seoul City Hospital for Orphans. The hospital provided 40 beds for children up to the age of ten. The squadron medical officer was appointed as the officer-in-charge of the project and the squadron sought to provide food and clothes, including items sourced from Australia and flown in on RAAF aircraft.

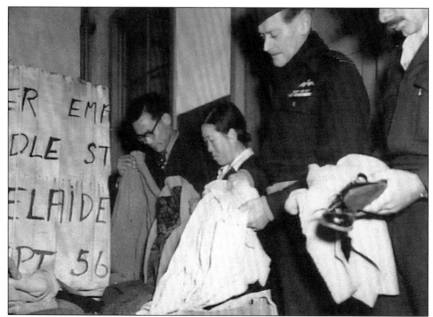

Unpacking one of the many cases of warm clothing sent to the Orphan Children's Hospital in Seoul following an appeal run by Hoyts Ozone Theatre Circuit in Adelaide. Present is Wing Commander Jack Kinninmont, then Commanding Officer of No 77 Squadron. (Australian War Memorial)

Throughout their service in Korea, the non-commissioned pilots of the RAAF had been met with some confusion by their USAF compatriots, where all pilots were officers. It had also led to issues regarding access to the American officers' social facilities, although these issues were conveniently managed by both their hosts and the Australians. Sergeant Colin King had his rank mistaken when socialising with the Americans:

> … More than half the squadron pilots were non-commissioned. There were a few warrant officers but mainly we were sergeants and a few flight sergeants. And the Americans couldn't handle that. They couldn't understand anything other than officer pilot.
>
> Now we were to do our messing with them. So what were we going to do? So, the RAAF came up with a simple solution. We took all our rank badges off and we just had our wings and a name tag.
>
> And my name tag was COL KING. So I got 'colonel' from all the Yanks. I was quite happy to run with that.

More significant was that Australian sergeant pilots often led missions that contained officers, and frequently more than one. Of 116 missions flown through August, 48 were led by seven different non-commissioned officers. Most notably, Col King was the leader on nine missions, while Flight Sergeant Tom Stoney, on his second tour, led 22. On one such mission, five of the eight Meteors led by Stoney were flown by officers.

The jet war in Korea had introduced many new variables that even long-term fighter pilots had not encountered, such as the high speeds associated with Meteor operations at low level and navigating over the rugged terrain in less-than-ideal weather conditions. Officers new to the squadron frequently flew their first few missions with a sergeant pilot leading, allowing them to gain valuable insights before leading in their own right; relevant experience was of more value than rank in seeking to operate successfully and survive.

Even with such measures in place, within a matter of weeks, a further three pilots and an engineering officer were killed. Flight Lieutenant LC 'Slim' Haslope had served with No 466 Squadron RAAF and survived flying Handley Page Halifax bombers over Europe during the Second World War. Three weeks after arriving in Korea, he was killed when his Meteor crashed on take-off. Also newly arrived, one of the RAF pilots, Flying Officer Olaf Bergh, was seen to eject from his burning aircraft at 6,000 feet as he climbed away following a strike on four machine-gun pits. Bergh was seen on the ground and became the only RAF prisoner-of-war during the Korean conflict.

On 1 September, Pilot Officer Alan Avery and his passenger, engineering officer Flight Lieutenant Henry Johnston, were ferrying a two-seat Meteor T.7 from Iwakuni to Kimpo in company with Flying Officer Randall 'Randy' Green in a single-seat F.8. The weather had been forecast as fine for the arrival at Kimpo with a stratiform layer of cloud en route. Avery was leading the two aircraft in formation when, climbing through 20,000 feet, the cloud darkened. The pair of Meteors then encountered extreme turbulence just as Green was about to advise Avery he could no longer hold formation. Having stalled, the two Meteors fell away, with Green entering a spin. He was able to recover control of his aircraft as it passed through 14,000 feet by applying full power and climbing away. He emerged from the cloud at 26,000 feet. Now in clear air, Green saw the cause of the event – a single, lone thunderstorm towering to 40,000 feet. Green limped back to Iwakuni, his aircraft severely damaged by hail and turbulence.

Avery and Johnston did not survive the encounter, having attempted to bale out just prior to the aircraft crashing into the sea. Their bodies were recovered in the days that followed. Unlike the F.8, the trainer did not possess ejection seats. Additionally, the canopy was of a greenhouse style and hinged along one edge, rather than sliding back, making egress difficult in an emergency.

Taken from the rear seat of a two-seat Meteor T.7, the Korean landscape is visible below as the aircraft follows Meteor F.8s conducting a ground attack mission. (Unknown

At this time, four pilots led hazardous missions against heavy anti-aircraft fire that contributed to their award of the Distinguished Flying Cross. Flight Lieutenant Eric Ramsay led a strike on a supply depot, also destroying a small bridge. Flying Officer AR 'Dick' Turner led what was reported as 'The most successful Napalm rocket strike carried out by Meteors to date', destroying supply buildings and a power transformer. Flight Lieutenant Doug Hurst led a rocket attack that destroyed 24 buildings and Flying Officer Alan 'Blue' Philp's formation landed 90 per cent of their rockets in the target area to destroy a few buildings, vehicles and supply shelters.

October 1952 saw the peace negotiations in Panmunjom suspended again and the Meteors providing escorts for USAF B-26 bombers. The Meteors operated below 20,000 feet and could observe the attack and withdrawal by the bombers below. MiG-15s were sighted but rarely engaged. They attacked four Meteors flying at 20,000 feet on 2 October with substantial effect. One aircraft was seen with an engine trailing smoke, which was subsequently shut down, and, in company with another Meteor, and low on fuel, departed the area. The pair both successfully landed on an emergency airstrip on a beach at Paengyong-Do with no further damage to the aircraft.

USAF B-26 Invader medium bombers on the flight line. (Alan Royston)

The other pair was engaged and a 37-mm cannon shell struck the tailpipe of the left engine of Sergeant Ken Murray's A77-446, causing him to shut down the damaged engine. Murray made it back to Kimpo, with the operating engine flaming out due to fuel starvation as he approached the airfield. The other Meteor was flown by Flying Officer Oliver Cruickshank (RAF), however, Murray lost sight of Cruickshank after the initial break from the attacking MiGs. The RAF pilot reported he was also low on fuel and heading for Ch'odo. After both engines had flamed out, Cruickshank had attempted to eject but was too low; an American rescue aircraft, callsign *Dumbo*, witnessed the aircraft and the seat impact the water in two separate splashes, but no parachute was seen. Oliver Cruickshank was posthumously mentioned in despatches.

Murray had returned for a second tour and A77-446 was his regular aircraft, with his nickname 'Black Murray' painted beneath the cockpit. Murray would go on to fly the most missions during the Korean War – 333. His service in Korea, and his subsequent career, would see him decorated with the rare combination of the Distinguished Flying Cross, Air Force Cross and Distinguished Flying Medal, in addition to the US Air Medal.

A Meteor raises its landing gear swiftly after take-off as it departs on another mission. (Unknown)

The squadron set about preparing for another Korean winter. Wooden crates were made into walkways and personnel watched films titled 'Survival in the Arctic'. Winter clothing arrived and ground crews readied for the difficulties in servicing the Meteors in freezing conditions. Even so, water pipes froze and burst, and crews kept their pot-belly stoves stoked within their tents for warmth and cooking meals. During his October 2003 Australians at War Film Archive recording, Sergeant, later Air Vice-Marshal, Bill Collings related the conditions the ground crews worked under:

> The ground crew had the worst part of it in winter, we were on perforated steel plate matting, you know, PSP, in sandbag revetments but if it had been snowing or whatever and they had to clean the snow off or if they got clear ice on it, it was so cold they'd burn themselves if they didn't wear gloves.

> So they had to clean the aeroplanes down and get rid of all the ice and they [had] a really awful job, particularly very early in the morning.

October 1952 had seen a further 700 missions flown by the squadron and, significantly, the total had surpassed 10,000 since the Meteor had been introduced in July 1951. Amid the adverse weather, operations continued, striking tunnels, buildings, trucks and rail installations. Maximum-effort missions saw 16 Meteors escorting USAF B-26 bombers at altitude, or delivering rocket strikes at low level. On one rocket attack in poor weather, Flight Lieutenant Ken Godfrey's aircraft lost a substantial section of its port nacelle; it was suspected to be the result of blast damage from the strike. November drew to a close with a visit from the Minister for Navy and Air, Mr William McMahon, who was destined to rise to the office of prime minister.

The RAAF engineers worked tirelessly to maintain the aircraft to a high operational standard. (George Hale)

On the evening of 12 December, a red alert sounded and squadron members moved to their defensive positions in battle equipment. The anti-aircraft batteries opened up, firing into the night sky at the unidentified intruder. The pilots were able to return to their tents an hour after midnight, but the alert would not end fully until four in the morning.

Christmas Eve saw the loss of Flight Lieutenant Frederick Lawrenson DFC AFC. He was leading an armed reconnaissance when, at 1,500 feet, his starboard wing exploded, sending the aircraft tumbling into a hillside.

Lawrenson was the final loss for 1952. Despite the freezing conditions, the squadron attempted to see in the New Year in the aircrew and ground crew clubs, entertaining their American guests who shared K14.

Over the preceding year, the squadron had first flown in the ground-attack role in January and gone on to fly a diverse range of missions that included a return to fighter sweeps. The ground war remained in a state of stalemate as peace negotiations continued to falter. The new year would see No 77 Squadron continue in its ground-attack role and register its final air-to-air victory of the Korean War.

Chapter 14
OF VICTORY AND LOSS

The deep freeze had set in again at Kimpo and 1953 commenced with a day without flying for No 77 Squadron and a winter lull in fighting on the ground. The weather continued to intervene throughout January, although it paved the way for a larger ice rink to be built at Kimpo. The month also saw the command of the squadron pass from Wing Commander Kinninmont to Wing Commander John Hubble, the former having completed his operational tour of Korea. Hubble, having arrived weeks earlier, had already flown and led several missions and was well versed in squadron operations. He continued to fly missions throughout his subsequent tour, including operations led by sergeant pilots.

The new year re-equipped pilots with hard-shell helmets, commonly referred to as 'bone domes'. While the American pilots had been flying with the new-style helmets throughout the war, the Australians had continued to employ the soft leather or canvas helmets, reminiscent of the Second World War.

Another critical difference in the pilots' equipment was that the American F-86 Sabre pilots wore 'G-suits'. In the intense manoeuvring of fighter-jet operations, the body is subjected to multiple forces of gravity, forcing the pilot down into the seat. The physiological effect of these G-forces is for oxygenated blood to migrate toward the lower body, depriving the brain of adequate supply and potentially resulting in the pilot blacking out. Pulling out from a rocket attack was one such manoeuvre that could cause this. The American G-suits consisted of a pair of outer pants that contained bladders that automatically expanded under the force of multiple gravities, thereby trapping the blood in the upper body and head. Like the Australians, the MiG-15 pilots did not wear hard helmets or G-suits.

Pilot numbers continued to be a challenge for the squadron and were assisted by the arrival of more Royal Air Force (RAF) exchange pilots in the form of Flying Officers Booth and Price. Meteor A77-15 was flown by Francis Booth on 27 January. It was an aircraft that had escaped two close calls in the past and had been the Meteor flown by Flying Officer Bruce Gogerly when he was initially credited with the first Royal Australian Air Force (RAAF) MiG kill of the war. Sadly, on the 27th, Booth was listed as missing in action as he carried out a rocket attack on trains at the entrances to two tunnels in the Sinmak region.

Throughout the conflict, several RAAF pilots returned for their second operational tours, while all recorded significant mission numbers beyond 100 over nine months. During that time, pilots would receive two weeks' leave in Japan and be accommodated at the Kawana Hotel. RAAF tours were subsequently reduced to six months but, while USAF pilots were typically limited to 100 missions per tour, this limit did not formally exist for the Australians. In a newspaper article as far back as the previous June, the Minister for Navy and Air,

William McMahon, denied reports the pilots were being overworked and were limited to the shorter of 100 missions or nine months. The same article noted the return of Sergeant Phillip Zupp, who had flown 201 missions in a single tour.

In January 1953, Flight Lieutenant Wal Rivers DFC and Bar held the record for the most missions in Korea with 319. Rivers had been with the squadron at the outbreak of the war, flying the second mission with Wing Commander Lou Spence as they escorted American B-26 bombers to strike at rail bridges. Having completed a tour on Mustangs, Rivers returned and flew a full second tour on Meteors to see his tally exceed 300.

Rivers' record fell on 17 February 1953 when Flight Sergeant Ken 'Black' Murray flew his 320th mission, leading a maximum-effort mission of 16 Meteors, escorting B-26 bombers. Murray would complete his tour with 333 missions, a record for any pilot under the United Nations Command in Korea.

Flight Sergeant Ken Murray following his 300th mission. He would go on to fly 333 missions – the most of any pilot in United Nations Command. (Australian War Memorial)

As February merged into March, events conspired to offer some hope of peace. The ongoing sticking point of the voluntary repatriation of prisoners eased slightly when both sides agreed to an exchange of sick and wounded prisoners of war. What would be known as Operation *Little Switch* was a preliminary measure towards a full prisoner exchange and the possibility of peace. The death of the Soviet leader Josef Stalin on 5 March further encouraged the chances of an armistice.

March also proved to be one of the most eventful months of the war for No 77 Squadron on several counts. On the 16th, one of the unit's most successful missions of the entire war was flown. The previous evening, Warrant Officer Bob Turner had been part of an attack on enemy vehicles to the south of Wonsan and the following morning returned to the area as the leader of a pair of Meteors. Surprisingly, the vehicles were not only still in the area but had an estimated 100 more lined up behind them. Turner and his wingman, Sergeant Dave Irlam, set about halting any chance of escape by attacking the trucks at the front and rear of the column. The other pair of the original formation, Flight Lieutenant Vince Hill and Sergeant Bill Collings, arrived from attacking vehicles elsewhere and proceeded to strafe the column. Now trapped, the trucks fell victim to multiple missions by the Meteors throughout the day with additional strikes by American aircraft. By day's end, it was estimated 90 trucks had been destroyed.

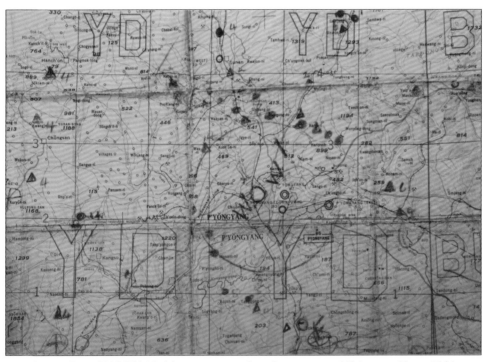

Sergeant George Hale's 'Flak Map' showing anti-aircraft emplacements around P'yŏngyang. (George Hale)

Another success for the squadron came on 27 March when Sergeant George Hale, flying Meteor A77-851, claimed an aerial victory over a MiG-15 in what was to be the final such victory for the RAAF. Hale was flying his regular aircraft with 'Halestorm' and a map of Tasmania painted beneath the cockpit. As one of four Meteors led by Wing Commander John Hubble, Hale was flying lead in a pair with Dave Irlam when they sighted and dived upon two MiG-15s that were pursuing two American jets, only to be attacked themselves by two additional MiGs. These enemy fighters almost overshot the Australian pair but not before severely damaging Irlam's aircraft.

Pursuing the pair, Hale dropped his ventral tank, and extended his air brakes to slow down, the two opposing pilots looking squarely at each other. Hale then positioned the MiG in front of him, 'clipped' its wings in the graticule of his gunsight and opened fire. The MiG belched smoke, with pieces falling from its fuselage, and rolled over into a steep dive as a third pair of enemy fighters entered the fray from the right. Hale landed hits on one aircraft of this pair, leaving it streaming white vapour before it made its escape. Out of ammunition and with Irlam's aircraft sporting more than 100 bullet holes, the pair descended to low level to return to base. Hale was credited with one destroyed and another probable. On his return, the ground crew painted the silhouettes of two MiGs near the existing nose art of A77-851. However, Hubble ordered the markings be painted over (these silhouettes were rediscovered decades later when the surviving nose section of *Halestorm* was being stripped back for restoration).

Crew Chief Bob Cherry poses with his 'kill markings' before they were ordered to be removed. This is believed to be the only photo taken while the markings were in place. (George Hale)

The nose of *Halestorm*, A77-851, after its aerial victory on 27 March 1953, with 'M.I.G. KILLER' written near the gun ports. (George Hale)

Throughout the war, the success of the interdiction campaign had been hampered by the North Korean and Chinese ability to repair damage in all too short a time. Successful strikes against the main supply route, bridges, roads and rail lines by day, could see repairs made overnight. However, this also led to concentrations of trucks and troops between damaged sections, providing targets for night bombing raids by B-26 bombers and a spate of night armed-reconnaissance flights by No 77 Squadron.

The nocturnal missions called for the pilots to be very proficient in flying with reference to their instruments in the absence of a visible horizon. A number of the RAF pilots were suitably qualified. The weather also needed to be favourable and the phase of the moon considered. Only a limited number of squadron pilots were qualified and proficient, one of whom was Wing Commander Hubble who led the first night mission in the Meteor on 21 March. Four aircraft would depart at 20-minute intervals and would receive vectors to the target area by a ground controller, or a series of controllers. On sighting lights below, they would attack the target.

On the first mission, Hubble sighted 30 lights in Sariwon that were quickly switched off on his approach before he fired a single rocket. Three more rockets were fired at Haeju, and lights, suspected to be headlamps, were strafed in a valley near Singye. The night obscured the ability to assess the damage, although Hubble rated the first night mission as 'very successful' on his return.

On one sortie, the flak seemed to be excessively heavy until the reason was discovered. One of the aircraft had inadvertently left its downward pointing identification light illuminated. Twenty night missions were flown during March but were not continued the following month.

The success of the first months of 1953 was countered by the losses sustained. Following Frank Booth's failure to return in January, there had been a heavy toll. Flight Sergeant John Halley crashed during a strafing attack near Sinmak on 11 February. Hubble's deputy commanding officer, Flight Lieutenant Don Hillier, was posted as missing in action after a rocket attack upon an armoured fighting vehicle on 8 March. Three weeks later, Sergeant Peter Chalmers was seen to crash into a small hill, having streamed fuel and then thick black smoke after attacking a truck south of Wonsan. On the 28th, Flying Officer Arthur Rosser (RAF) was posted as missing in action, having also attacked trucks in the Wonsan area.

Since the war had erupted on 25 June 1950, No 77 Squadron had lost one of its engineering staff in a flying accident and 35 pilots, including those who died in the tragic tent fire in the winter of 1950. When the planned squadron complement was 24 pilots and a maximum-effort mission considered to be 16 Meteors, such losses were high and even greater on a personal level. Yet as the peace talks reconvened at Panmunjon in April 1953, there was no apparent easing of operations as air power was considered a substantial element of continued pressure in achieving a negotiated peace.

Final Encounter by digital artist Mark Donoghue.

HALESTORM
SERGEANT GEORGE HALE

Tasmanian-born, Sergeant George Hale's Gloster Meteor F.8 wore a map of the Apple Isle beneath the rim of its cockpit when he served with No 77 Squadron RAAF in Korea. Appropriately, the name 'Halestorm' also appeared on the aircraft that was officially marked as A77-851 and would go into history as the last RAAF aircraft to score a victory in an air-to-air engagement.

George Hale (left) briefing his brother, Corporal Vernon Hale of the Commonwealth Division, before a practice flight in a Meteor T.7. (Australian War Memorial)

Hale had graduated 'Dux' of his pilot's course at Point Cook, Victoria, and subsequently converted onto the de Havilland Vampire jet fighter at Williamtown, New South Wales. He was trained on the Gloster Meteor at Iwakuni, Japan, in late 1952 in preparation for his active service in Korea, where No 77 Squadron was primarily involved in ground-attack duties, rocket strikes and bomber escorts, as well as armed and road-reconnaissance missions.

On 27 March 1953, Hale was flying one of four Meteors led by Wing Commander John Hubble. Hale was flying lead in a pair with Sergeant Dave Irlam when they sighted and dived on two MiG-15s pursuing two American jets, only to be attacked themselves by two additional MiG-15s. These enemy fighters almost overshot the Australian pair but not before severely damaging Irlam's aircraft. Realising he was in for a fight, Hale dropped his ventral tank and slipped in between the pair of MiGs. He then fired two rockets that passed between the MiGs, sending them to port and starboard. Hale followed the aircraft to port.

The MiG extended its speedbrakes to slow down, as did Hale and the two pilots looked squarely at each other. The MiG then attempted to accelerate away. As the MiG pulled ahead, the Meteor pilot opened fire. The MiG belched smoke, shed pieces of its fuselage and rolled over into a steep dive as a third pair of enemy fighters entered the fray from his right.

Hale turned to the incoming aircraft which attempted to pull up and away. Running out of energy with his nose skyward, the Meteor was on the verge of stalling when he opened fire. He saw flashes on the MiG's wing root as the shells landed, leaving it streaming white vapour before it made its escape. Hale flew a stall turn and descended away. Out of ammunition, and with Irlam's aircraft sporting more than 100 bullet holes, the pair flew at low-level and returned to Kimpo.

Sergeant George Hale inspecting battle damage. (George Hale)

Later, Hale was credited with one 'kill' and one 'probable' and a ground crew member added the silhouettes of two MiGs beneath 'Halestorm' near the cockpit of A77-851.

Sergeant George Hale
A35090
No 77 Squadron RAAF
Korea 1952–53

Meteor A77851 'Halestorm' (Juanita Franzi)

Gloster Meteor A77-851 was built for the RAF as WK683 but was delivered directly to Japan. In early 2022, its cockpit and forward fuselage were donated to the RAAF by the South Australian Aviation Museum.

Chapter 15
TOWARDS THE ARMISTICE

The squadron had received some good news earlier in the year when a Christmas card was received from Flight Lieutenant Gordon Harvey who had been a prisoner of war for more than two years since he belly landed his Mustang in January 1951. Only in recent months had prisoners in North Korea been permitted any form of communication home in the form of letters or cards. As the parties debated how to bring about peace for the first time since negotiations collapsed in October 1952, the pace of operations at Kimpo did not subside.

The losses in preceding weeks and the heavy anti-aircraft fire in the area of operations had moved Wing Commander Hubble to issue a directive to his pilots. It outlined that reconnaissance would be flown at a higher altitude, only single passes were to be made on targets and groups of less than four vehicles were not to be attacked as they likely represented a flak trap. The benefits of natural assets such as terrain and the sun to enhance the element of surprise were reaffirmed, just as they had been by leaders since the dawn of fighter tactics.

Briefing before another mission over Korea. (Alan Royston)

Rocket strikes remained in full force with the Meteors receiving new rocket rails to enable the aircraft to carry 16 rockets, double the previous striking power. During one strike upon a power station on 7 April, another RAF pilot was reported missing, believed killed. The Meteor of Flying Officer RL 'Jimmy' James was seen to slowly roll twice after the attack before crashing, inverted, into a mud flat.

Late April was marked by incessant raids by 'Bedcheck Charlie' and the return of Wing Commander Cresswell for two weeks. The former commanding officer was on a fact-finding mission and observed the Meteor in the ground-attack role firsthand, flying five missions. He was suitably impressed with the Meteor's performance in the role it had subsequently adopted. On his return to Australia, Cresswell took command of the reformed No 2 Operational Training Unit at RAAF Williamtown, where pilots were prepared for jet combat operations before they arrived in Korea.

The previous lack of such transitional training had been a key element in Cresswell sending 11 pilots home during his tenure in command. He later stated he did not blame the pilots sent home but the system that sent them to Korea poorly trained and without instrument ratings that enabled them to safely fly and navigate in cloud.

Interdiction missions by 16 aircraft continued in earnest, routinely reporting between 100 and 150 rockets striking the chosen target area of buildings, trucks or troop concentrations. RAF pilot, Flying Officer George Dollittle, was one of four Meteors making a rocket attack against troop concentrations near Haeju, on 17 May. Dollittle failed to pull out of a dive after releasing his rockets. An explosion was seen on a small hill following the attack and a low pass by another Meteor identified parts of an aircraft. The pilot was not seen to eject.

Officers of No 77 Squadron with members of No 36 Squadron, which had delivered supplies of rockets and aircraft spares from Japan. (Australian War Memorial)

May saw the return of night reconnaissance missions by four armed Meteors and, again, Wing Commander Hubble was active in their execution. Vehicles provided the most common target, their headlamps gaining attention, although on one occasion a searchlight was extinguished by the rockets and cannons of a Meteor. As before, the night missions were flown by the limited cadre of pilots suitably qualified to fly on instruments at night.

June began with the coronation of Queen Elizabeth II on the third day of the month. Meteors had previously flown to Iwakuni to participate in celebrations over Japan, while the newly renamed No 36 Squadron (previously No 30 Transport Unit until 10 March 1953) had flown officers and non-commissioned officers to take part on the ground. At Kimpo, a partial stand-down was called with no missions being flown. Instead, an unofficial test match was played between a No 77 Squadron team and members of the United States Air Force (USAF) on the latter's baseball diamond. The squadron clerk provided commentary over the public address system to the several hundred servicemen that had gathered; while several American batsmen impressed, the art of overarm bowling was a lesser feature of their play.

Six-year-old Kim Meon Sikieh, who lived in a village near Kimpo, with Flying Officer John Alford. (Australian War Memorial)

June 4 saw the Communists accept the majority of the United Nations Command proposals. The following day saw the handover of command of the squadron from Wing Commander John Hubble to Wing Commander Alan Hodges AFC. Hodges had already flown several missions since his arrival and, although he was unaware of it at the time, he was to be the final Commanding Officer of No 77 Squadron during the hostilities of the Korean War. A week later, Sergeant Desmond Nolan was killed during air-to-air training near Kimpo when his Meteor was seen to shed pieces, while recovering from a barrel roll and dive, before crashing into the ground.

June 15 was a significant day with the squadron flying 88 sorties for the day, Hodges flying five. In the execution of these, Sergeant Donald Pinkstone ejected when his Meteor was hit by flak and caught fire. At low altitude, the chances of a successful ejection were minimal, but Pinkstone had the presence of mind to release his seat harness in advance of being punched out of his Meteor. This minimised the time until he was clear of the seat and able to deploy his parachute. Even so, he was fired upon during his descent into a paddy field where he gathered up his parachute and made his way to a small hill to set off an orange flare. Resembling the plight of Sergeant Ces Sly in 1951, the American rescue helicopter sent to rescue Pinkstone was repelled by ground fire. Unlike, Sly's rescue, there was no second helicopter and the sergeant pilot became the sixth and final No 77 Squadron pilot to be taken prisoner during the war.

In the weeks that followed, two pilots were fortunate to escape a similar fate. Sergeant WD 'Bill' Monaghan had a close call when he was hit by ground fire during a rocket attack. A huge hole was ripped through the starboard nacelle, disabling the engine. Flying on the remaining engine, Monaghan limped out to sea and away from enemy lines, ultimately landing safely at the emergency airstrip on Paengyong-Do.

Flying Officer John Coleman (RAF) thanks the crew of the USAF rescue helicopter, a Sikorsky H-5, that picked him up within an hour of ejecting from his stricken Meteor. (Australian War Memorial)

Flying Officer John Coleman was climbing away from an attack on a heavily defended target when he felt a bump. His throttles were jammed, hydraulics were lost, and he was without an airspeed indicator or radio. Managing to fly far enough south to be over friendly territory, Coleman ejected and was picked up by a USAF rescue helicopter and returned to Kimpo within the hour.

The Americans and Australians worked closely in search-and-rescue operations, particularly for downed pilots. The American helicopter crews were valiant in their efforts to recover airmen, often under intense ground fire. Similarly, the Australians were frequently called to cover the rescue of Allied pilots, flying combat air patrols to ward off enemy fighters as the recovery took place below.

July provided a mixture of armed reconnaissances, rocket strikes and days grounded due to poor weather. The war appeared to be drawing to a close, but the United Nations Command aircraft sustained a significant effort regardless as a final counteroffensive to the enemy's movement was launched. On 16 July, four Meteors were scrambled to attack a series of boxcars. Flying as number four in the formation, on attachment to the squadron from No 91 Wing, Squadron Leader Leonard McGlinchey's Meteor rolled and crashed on take-off. His aircraft exploded, the full load of fuel and weapons igniting.

No cause was determined, although reports of puffs of smoke from an engine were forthcoming with suspicions of engine failure; however, suggestions of a thrown tyre tread striking and damaging a wing flap may have caused the aircraft to roll. Regardless of the reason, the unfortunate reality was that Squadron Leader McGlinchey would be recorded as No 77 Squadron's final pilot loss during the Korean War.

Eleven days later, four Meteors flew the squadron's final mission of the war. Flying his 100th mission, Pilot Officer Geoff Collins led newly arrived Sergeants Doel, Millis and Rees on an uneventful familiarisation flight to Ch'odo Island, Paengyong-Do and home to Kimpo for the final time.

On 27 July 1953, the No 77 Squadron Unit History Sheet simply states:

> At 1001 hours today, the Korean Armistice was officially signed between Allied Officers and Communist Officers at PANMUNJON and the ceasefire was effected from 2200 hours the same day.

After three years and nearly 19,000 missions, the squadron's active service in the Korean War had drawn to a close. The Armistice was met with mixed feelings by the pilots as Sergeant John Seaton recalled when filmed for the Australians at War Film Archive:

> One or two perhaps were elated that – well, we were all elated – it's hard to explain. It's a lot of fun being associated with a good war, particularly if you're flying. I don't know about the Army blokes, I don't think they look at it the same way.

> But it's very difficult to explain, you are elated that things finish in a way, but it's very exciting though – doing a trip like the ones that we used to do.

The squadron was witness to a MiG-15 encounter one last time on 21 September when a North Korean pilot, No Kum So, landed at Kimpo, having defected with his aircraft in response to US$100,000 and asylum being offered for such a defection.

No 77 Squadron had left Darwin bound for Milne Bay, New Guinea, in February 1943 and had been on deployment overseas for more than a decade. The squadron would remain overseas until November 1954, moving to a base at Kunsan in March. It lost one more pilot during its peacetime service before returning home. Pilot Officer Harry Andrews was killed when his Meteor, A77-866, collided with another while conducting formation flying practice at 15,000 feet. The other pilot ejected and survived.

Led by Squadron Leader McNamara, the Meteors of No 77 Squadron perform a formation flypast of Seoul following the Armistice. (Ted Jones)

At home, the Korean War was in the newspapers but, for the majority of the greater public, the conflict was not something generally considered. Fifty-two years later, when interviewed for the Australians at War Film Archive, Flying Officer Phil Hamilton-Foster recalled his return to Australia in 1952:

> I don't think a lot of people knew there was a war going on. You know, the average person in the street would say, or you'd go into a pub and have a drink and say, 'I just got back from 77 Squadron Korea.'
>
> They'd say, 'Where's Korea?'
>
> See because it didn't concern a lot of people because it was the forgotten war as they say. If you weren't involved in it personally well then, you know, why worry?

On 10 November 1954, 41 Meteors and 1,200 tons of equipment began loading on board HMAS *Vengeance* for the long journey home. The ship departed Yokosuka for Manus Island, and ultimately Sydney, arriving on 3 December. On entering Sydney Harbour, the squadron received a flypast of 12 DH Vampire jets of No 2 Operational Training Unit in the form of a 'Double Seven', appropriately led by Wing Commander Dick Cresswell.

The final chapter took place in the opening months of 1955 when Operation *Welcome Home* involved 16 Gloster Meteor F.8s formed up in a 'Double Seven' formation and, as part of the celebration, overflew several of the capital cities. For a month, commencing on 15 January, the Meteors flew over Canberra, Melbourne, Adelaide, Perth, Hobart and Brisbane before concluding the tour overhead Sydney. Many of the pilots were veterans of the Korean War and, like their squadron, were finally home.

Meteors at rest, 27 July 1953. The Armistice is signed. (Australian War Memorial)

OPERATION *MOOLAH*

The United Nations Command forces had long wanted to see the MiG-15 up close to study the swept-wing jet in detail since it had first appeared in the skies over Korea in 1950. In early 1953, Operation *Moolah* was put into action through propaganda leaflets offering a reward of US$100,000 and political asylum to any MiG-15 pilot who defected to South Korea with a mission-capable example of the aircraft.

The Russian-built MiG-15 piloted by North Korean pilot Lieutenant No Kum Sok (or No Kum So) shortly after he landed the aircraft at Kimpo, on 21 September 1953, and surrendered the aircraft to United Nations forces. (Australian War Memorial)

The plan had been hatched before the Armistice in July and, to the surprise of all involved, a lone MiG-15 made an approach to land at K14 Kimpo on 21 September 1953, waggling its wings and firing distress flares. It touched down in the opposite direction to landing Sabres, narrowly avoiding a collision. Climbing from his cockpit, Lieutenant No Kum So was met by Allied pilots with their pistols drawn before being rushed to Fifth Air Force Headquarters for questioning. Unsure of what was taking place, fighters were scrambled but met no further MiGs.

The aircraft was subsequently dismantled and shipped to Kadena Air Base on Okinawa where it was repainted in US markings and flown through a series of trials. Three of these flights, totalling nearly three hours, were flown by Major Charles 'Chuck' Yeager, who was noted as the first person through the sound barrier in level flight, flying the Bell X-1 in 1947. Yeager was confronted by instruments calibrated under the Metric system and found the aircraft to be dangerously uncontrollable at Mach 0.98, approaching supersonic flight.

North Korean pilot Lieutenant No Kum Sok (or No Kum So) wearing his flying gear. (Australian War Memorial)

No Kum So, who had apparently defected without knowledge of the reward, emigrated to the United States, where he became a US citizen and worked for major aerospace companies under the name Kenneth Rowe.

Chapter 16
HEAVY LIFTING

Originally carrying a red stripe along the fuselage and '77 Squadron' in red above the cabin windows, two Douglas C-47 Dakota aircraft and their crews had served in Japan with the British Commonwealth Occupation Force (BCOF). Along with two small, single-engine Taylorcraft Austers, the four machines constituted the Communications Flight of No 77 Squadron based at Iwakuni. With the outbreak of the Korean War on 25 June 1950, and the squadron's entrance into the conflict soon after, the unit transitioned from a basic communications flight into a fully-fledged squadron.

Changing its name to No. 30 Communications Flight, the Dakotas now provided a vital supply line between Japan and Korea as the Mustangs increasingly transited airfields on the peninsula. As the battle for the Pusan Perimeter raged through August and September 1950, the Dakotas were tasked with flying desperately needed ammunition and supplies into Taegu airfield as No 77 Squadron flew close air support missions to a battle front only minutes away. It was dangerous for the crews of the relatively slow, twin-engine transport aircraft loaded with explosive cargo as they flew down valleys within reach of North Korean artillery and under enemy fire.

The tireless efforts of RAAF ground crews were pivotal in the RAAF's contribution during the conflict. Here, engineers service the engine of a Dakota of No 30 Transport Unit. (Australian War Memorial)

Dakota A65-96

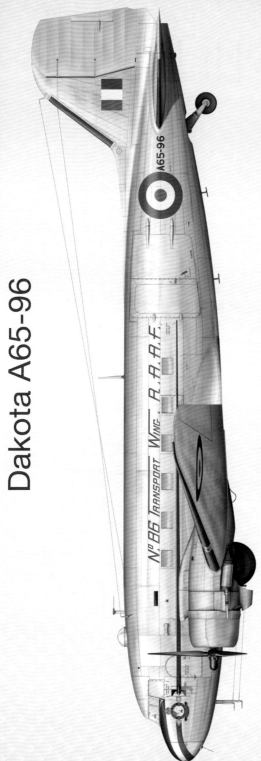

Douglas C-47B Dakota (Juanita Franzi)

During the early part of the Korean War, A65-96 was deployed to Japan and came under No 91 Wing, flying courier and transport flights into Korea. Its typical post–Second World War 'No. 86 Transport Wing R.A.A.F.' legend changed to 'Royal Australian Air Force' in 1951. It also had the upper fuselage and fin painted white around this time.

TECHNICAL DATA

DESCRIPTION:

Military transport with crew of three or four. Capacity up to 28 troops or 18 stretchers or 3,400 kg (7,500 lb) of freight. All-metal stressed-skin construction.

POWER PLANTS:

Two 895-kW (1,200-hp) Pratt & Whitney Twin Wasp R-1830-92 radial piston engines.

DIMENSIONS:

Span 28.95 m (95 ft); length 19.62 m (64 ft 5 in); height 5.15 m (16 ft 11 in).

WEIGHTS:

Typical empty 8,250 kg (18,190 lb); max loaded 13,290 kg (29,300 lb).

PERFORMANCE:

Max speed 368 km/h (229 mph); normal cruising speed 280 km/h (174 mph); initial climb 353 m/min (1,160 ft/min); service ceiling 7,315 m (24,000 ft); normal range 2,414 km (1,500 miles).

With the official formation of the flight into No 30 Communication Unit under the command of Flight Lieutenant David Hitchins in November, the unit was still well below projected levels of staff although more C-47 Dakotas were en route. With an ideal establishment of 64 personnel, the unit had 20 – seven officers, ten non-commissioned officers and three airmen. Unlike No 77 Squadron, the unit did not fall under the command of the Americans' Fifth Air Force; rather, it remained under the BCOF. Additionally, the Dakotas received routine servicing from their own maintenance unit, with 100-hourly inspections and more significant work conducted by No 491 Maintenance Squadron. These tasks also fell to the in-house maintenance unit on occasions, however, when 491 Squadron was heavily committed with 77 Squadron battle damage and routine servicing.

Sergeant Frank Field, an electrical fitter, recalled some of the issues in maintaining the Dakotas when he was interviewed in April 2004:

> The airframe people had problems because of the weather conditions. The Dakotas had fabric covered ailerons, elevators and rudder and the fabric used to be stretched and made taut in the extreme cold conditions, but otherwise … the weather never adversely affected our serviceability rate any more than what it would have here in Australia.

> We were all vigilant as far as that was concerned, not only the airframe fitters and the aircrews but all technical musterings, particularly when we had the wings covered with snow covers in wintertime. We had to be particularly careful removing them, particularly if there was a lot of snow on them.

> And we didn't place too much weight on the fabric, otherwise you'd tear it. That rendered the aircraft unserviceable until it was repaired. But it was only the snow that made the role of airframe fitters more difficult than anybody else. We in the electrical game never had any problems other than what we'd strike anywhere [else].

Severe weather, including a typhoon, hampered operations as the C-47s endeavoured to support No 77 Squadron after its move northward to the frozen airfield at Hamhŭng. On 18 November 1950, four flights were made from Iwakuni to Hamhŭng totalling nearly 20 hours in the air for the crews. The airfield was positioned so close to the front line that departing Dakotas turned immediately after take-off to avoid flying into hostile airspace and the threat of ground fire. The last day of the month saw the first C-47 arrive from Singapore where it had served with No 90 Wing as part of the Malayan Emergency effort.

From 3 December, the unit was fully occupied over the following three days evacuating 77 Squadron from Hamhŭng to Pusan as the North Korean counteroffensive pushed the United Nations forces south again. Flights were also flown in the depths of winter to support the United States Air Force (USAF) and the British 27th and 29th Brigades as their air head had moved south to Suwon. At this time, the first Dakota A65-74 was lost in a ground accident at K13 Suwon. The aircraft was struck by a USAF F-51 Mustang as it climbed away after take-off, fortunately with no casualties being sustained. While no blame was attributed for the accident, the aircraft's cockpit was crushed and the Dakota was a write-off with all salvageable spares recovered and flown to Iwakuni. Luckily, the pilots seated in the cockpit suffered no injuries.

Operating in the severe winter environment came with additional hazards for the Dakotas. Ice build-up on the airframe of an aircraft spoils the streamlined shape of the wing that creates the lift, in addition to adding the weight of the frozen water. Despite anti-icing equipment on the wings, tails and propellers, the Dakotas would still have to fly with higher power settings to maintain flight at far slower speeds, carrying persistent ice build-ups they could not shed.

A further four Dakotas arrived with one being modified as a VIP aircraft and cast immediately into its purpose conveying the Commonwealth Commander-in-Chief, Lieutenant General Sir Horace Robertson KBE DSO, between Japan and Korea. The unit's complement of seven C-47s was challenged through December by both the weather and two aircraft that suffered engine failures. Another suffered damage at Yeongdeungpo when it dropped a wheel into an unmarked and poorly repaired bomb crater, striking both its wingtip and propeller blades. By this stage, while still supporting No 77 Squadron, the unit's role had broadened in support of the wider BCOF and its ground forces.

Soldiers of units and battalions of all British troops wait to board the waiting Douglas C47 dakota aircraft of no. 30 transport unit for the flight to Korea. (Australian War Memorial)

With the Taegu airfield in Korea becoming a central hub for all flight operations, the availability of fuel hampered the ability of the unit's aircraft to conduct their roundtrip flights from Japan. This resulted in a reduction in valuable lifting capacity that was normally available for personnel, freight and mail. As a consequence, approval was sought and granted to raise the maximum take-off weight of the Dakota from 27,000lb to 28,500lb (12,247kg to 12,927kg) for flights exceeding two and a half hours.

With the increased activity on the peninsula, the unit increased its involvement in the medical-evacuation role, flying 19 medevacs in December. The unit also utilised the two single-engine Austers when search missions were flown looking for the crew of a USAF light bomber that had gone missing in the Inland Sea (unfortunately without success).

As 1950 drew to a close, No 30 Communication Unit flew a different type of mission – Operation *Haggis*. This involved delivering 180lb (82kg) of haggis to the British troops of the Argyles and Sutherlands in Korea. Overall, the unit had been called upon to fly nearly 600 hours in the final month of the year. In December, its seven Dakotas had carried more than 1,500 passengers and 440,000lb (200 tonnes) of mail and freight between Japan and Korea, while their operations within Korea had carried almost 2,000 personnel and 250,000lb (113 tonnes) of freight.

January 1951 was welcomed with more bad weather. Mail, freight and personnel continued to be flown to the Korean Peninsula with Flight Lieutenant Noel Eliot captaining a flight to deliver 60 reinforcements to the Royal Ulster Rifles, while 1,430 medical cases were evacuated. In the poor weather, congestion was ever present at airfields and in the air as faster USAF Douglas C-54 Skymasters would depart close behind the RAAF transports and arrive overhead destinations in Korea simultaneously. With jet aircraft receiving priority in the take-off and landing sequences, delays both aloft and on the ground were exacerbated.

With the further withdrawal of ground forces, the unit's daily courier flights moved from terminating at K13 Suwon to the less desirable K5 Taejon. A basic earthen runway, Taejon resembled a ploughed paddock once it was wet and taxied upon by multiple aircraft. To worsen the situation, the earth would freeze overnight with the harsh ridges resulting in tyre failures. The terrain surrounding the airfield was also towering and inhospitable, often concealed in thick cloud. Consequently, the Dakotas operated down to a higher minimum altitude than that published by the USAF, as they sought to gain visual reference with the airfield. The length and condition of the runway also saw the Dakotas operate into the airfield with a reduced landing weight which again limited the amount of payload carried. Squadron Leader John Gerber arrived late in the month to assume command from David Hitchins who had commanded the Dakota operation from its fledgling days under No 77 Squadron through to the operational unit it had become.

February welcomed the eighth, and final Dakota to the unit and saw the British air head return to Suwon, removing all operations from Taejon. Throughout the month, more than a quarter of the Dakotas' flight time had the crews flying in cloud and on their instruments in contrast to 77 Squadron's fighter operations which were predominantly flown visually as few of their pilots were fully qualified in instrument flight. The Dakota crews flew five ground-controlled approaches in cloud in February with two only seeing the runway after breaking clear of cloud below 200 feet.

Morale remained high within the unit with the only issue reported being one of enthusiasm as Second Pilots (co-pilots) were clamouring to check out as captains in the left-hand seat. Gerber ensured training standards were maintained within the unit, particularly in flying the Dakota on one engine. This thoroughness proved beneficial as the unit's aircraft sustained three engine failures in February with Flight Lieutenant Alfred Tafe suffering the failure at the critical point of flight after take-off at Pusan. Tafe shut the engine down, feathered the propeller edge into the airflow to reduce drag and returned to land at Pusan.

The cockpit of a C47 Dakota. (Australian War Memorial)

The Battle of Kapyong commenced on 22 April 1951 and the demand for the unit's services grew rapidly to deliver troops, supplies and ammunition to a degree that it was estimated that 53 Dakotas would be required, far beyond the unit's establishment of eight. Consequently, the USAF assisted with more than 30 transports operating between Japan and Korea.

Amid the operations, one supply drop went awry when the Army called for the Dakota to drop its supplies on a red cross they had laid out, rather than the standard markings. Unfortunately, when the aircraft arrived, its crew sighted no less than 20 red crosses on the ground marking first aid stations and other various medical elements. Unable to distinguish the particular drop zone, Flight Lieutenant Cedric Thomas and his crew flew to Kimpo and unloaded the supplies.

At this time, the unit experienced its first casualty when one of the Austers crashed at Matsuyama, killing Sergeant Bernard Harding and his two passengers. The unit was fortunate not to lose its remaining Auster within days as it searched Hiroshima Bay, looking for a missing aircraft. Carrying a Very signalling pistol on board, the flare fired and set the fabric floor of the Auster alight. The pilot and his signaller made a hasty return to Iwakuni where the fire was fully extinguished and the aircraft subsequently repaired.

Through April, more than 100 missions were flown and over 600 hours accrued across seven pilots, co-pilots and navigators. Seven crew members had completed their ten-month operational tour and were returning to Australia, to be replaced by a similar number. Dave Hitchins had been with Communication Flight – 77 Squadron before its official inception in November 1950. Originally attached to an RAF Dakota Flight in Japan in 1947, he was the flight commander of the No 77 Squadron C-47 Dakotas at the outbreak of the war and flown numerous hazardous missions into Taegu during the battle of the Pusan Perimeter. He was also Lieutenant General Robertson's personal pilot.

When his time came to return to Australia in May 1951, Hitchins had been in Japan for more than four years and accumulated more than 100 missions to Korea and 1,500 hours flying the Dakota. Squadron Leader Gerber was high in praise for his predecessor and his substantial contribution.

As Hitchins departed, the unit's tasking increased as the 3rd Battalion, Royal Australian Regiment, introduced a leave cycle for soldiers that equated to an additional two Dakota flights each week to transfer men between Japan and Korea. This influx of soldiers to Japan meant that, through June, the unit flew 800 troops to Korea but 1,400 to Japan. Importantly, another 550 were medical evacuations, so the aircrews' hours remained high, 80 hours per month, and with 25% of flight time spent in cloud and flying on instruments.

In July 1951, CAC Wirraway A20-750 force landed at an emergency airstrip at Omru, to the north-east of Nagasaki. Flying Officer Ken Blight had become lost in bad weather and had overrun the airstrip, with the aircraft subsequently overturning. Except for a cut wrist to his passenger, there were no injuries although considerable damage saw the aircraft converted to components. The Wirraway had been an asset in providing instrument flying training instead of assigning a valuable Dakota to the task.

The unit flew nearly 700 hours in August, its second-highest total since its formation.

As with his counterparts at No 77 Squadron, John Gerber led from the front, routinely flying Dakota missions to Korea and air tests on aircraft after servicing. With Hitchins now in Australia, the commanding officer also flew the VIP flights. On 7 August, Gerber flew a supply-drop mission to British forces to the north of the Imjin and Hantan Chon river junction where the waters had risen rapidly and cut them off. In heavy rain, Gerber approached the first of two nominated drop zones, only to be waved off by the troops below, before he proceeded to the second drop zone and successfully delivered the supplies. The weather was a precursor to Typhoon *Marge* that moved into the region and cancelled flying to Korea. Even when the worst of the weather had passed, a number of flights to Pusan and Taegu still returned to Iwakuni without landing due to low cloud and rain at their destinations.

One of the more sobering duties that befell the unit was to convey funeral parties to Pusan for the burial of No 77 Squadron pilots. In August, a Dakota was flown by Warrant Officer Roy Rosevear for the burial of Flight Sergeant Reginald Lamb (RAF). Both units possessed crew on detachment from the Royal Air Force.

The start of October had seen the commander-in-chief of the British Forces in Korea change from Lieutenant General Sir Horace Robertson to Lieutenant General William Bridgeford. For the Dakotas, the end of October marked the end of the first year of operations since No 30 Communication Unit was formed. It completed the year with a record month, flying more hours (730) and evacuating more wounded (711). On a larger scale, its first 12 months of operations had involved 6,727 hours, 17,195 passengers and 4,268 medical evacuees. In addition, 1.32 million pounds (599 tonnes) of mail and 2.02 million pounds (916 tonnes) of freight had been carried by the eight Dakotas and their crews.

En route from Korea to Japan via Dakota are Flight Lieutenants Frank O'Leary (left) and Gordon Harvey following the latter's release from two-and-a-half years in captivity in North Korea. (Australian War Memorial)

Squadron Leader Gerber recognised the ability to meet the high workload was in no small way due to the efforts of the unit's maintenance team. Additionally, when Typhoon *Ruth* bore down on Iwakuni, the ground crews skilfully manoeuvred the Dakotas into the limited space available in the hangars. The typhoon grounded all operations other than a single medical evacuation flight flown by Flying Officer Wallace Pettersson who was able to fly to Kimpo and return before the winds became too strong.

November 5 saw the unit renamed No 30 Transport Unit, which was more in keeping with its significant role. Crews completing their tours returned to Australia via Qantas flights or Dakotas returning for major servicing, flying via Iwo Jima, Guam, Momote and Townsville. With new crews arriving, the squadron's remaining CAC Wirraway was utilised for instrument training. Pilots would fly navigation exercises on homing beacons and ground-controlled approaches in the two-seat, single-engine trainer.

In December, the British air head moved from Kimpo to K16 Yeongdeungpo, alleviating much of the congestion and many of the delays. Through the final month, crews averaged 109 hours of flight time, partly due to only five crews being available as others were struck down by severe colds in the depth of the winter. However, the healthy crews were given a reprieve on Christmas Day when a special freight flight was flown to Korea by Flight Lieutenant John Thomas to deliver mail to the troops and transport medical evacuees on return to Iwakuni. Squadron Leader Gerber closed out 1951 when he was forced to return to Kimpo following the failure of one of his Dakota's engines.

Chapter 17
STEADFAST SUPPORT

With their new name and a new year upon them, No 30 Transport Unit continued its routine of daily 'Army courier' flights, VIP transports, medical evacuations, and conveying troops to the battle and to Japan for rest and recuperation. With the change of role to ground attack for No 77 Squadron, a new task began to appear – 'Rocket Specials'. Considered too sensitive for transport by sea, the Dakotas were entrusted with delivering the 60-lb (27-kg) rocket heads to Kimpo and, in time, those filled with napalm.

A RAAF C-47 Dakota bearing 77 Squadron markings, before becoming No. 30 Communication Unit. (Dave Hitchins)

Illness persisted throughout the unit, reducing not only pilot numbers but the ability to implement the strategy of pairing inexperienced pilots with those experienced in operations throughout Japan and Korea. Maintenance also proved a challenge as the original planning for operating the Dakotas was forecast on 500 hours each month and the unit was consistently flying in the vicinity of 700 hours. Consequently, 100-hourly periodic maintenance fell due more frequently than originally envisioned.

As No 491 Maintenance Squadron was heavily engaged with No 77 Squadron – beyond the scheduled demands and battle damage, rocket rails had to be fitted to the Meteors to facilitate the ground-attack role and the envisioned target of 1,000 missions in a month – the maintenance section of No 30 Transport Unit was able to conduct some of the 100-hourly inspections, allowing the Dakotas to keep flying. Maintenance needs had also been assisted by the employment of skilled local Japanese labour, many of whom had acquired their training during the Second World War.

The pilots, navigators and signallers of the Dakotas were flying 100 hours each month and routinely completing their tours with more than 1,000 additional hours. In February, signaller Warrant Officer Neil Lang surpassed 1,000 hours, and received a Commendation for Meritorious Service in the Air, while pilot Flight Lieutenant Warwick Addison received the Air Force Cross, having accrued 1,493 hours. Crew were also returning for second tours, with those who had previously flown as second pilot gaining a captaincy. One such pilot was Flight Sergeant Leon Murtagh, who had been a pilot on the Dakota struck by the American F-51 Mustang and the pilot of the Auster which had its floor set alight by the Very flare. Ultimately, Murtagh would return to Japan a third time and complete his service with 338 flights to Korea. The month also saw the unit achieve a major milestone in passing one million miles flown since the outbreak of the Korean War.

In April, having completed more than a year in Japan, Squadron Leader John Gerber handed command to Squadron Leader Rodney Murdoch AFC and Bar. Ongoing training continued in earnest under Murdoch with practice instrument flying, navigation and ground-controlled approaches being flown in the Wirraway to supplement the operational flying in the Dakota. Instrument-rated pilots received a classification, the basic level being a 'White Card'. Normally assessed by flight tests and ground examinations, Murdoch provisionally upgraded two of his captains to a higher 'Green Card' level due to their real-world experience in severe weather over Japan and Korea.

June 1952 saw the unit suffer a fatality when Wirraway A20-745 struck telephone wires on a low-flying sortie. The pilot, Sergeant James Codd, was a second pilot on Dakotas; his passenger was Corporal Raymond Waddell, an instrument fitter with the unit. In conducting the flight, Sergeant Codd flew along the Hiji River near Nagahama before striking the wires that stretched across the river 70 feet (21 metres) above the water. Local Japanese citizens rescued the two airmen before they were conveyed to hospital where Codd was treated for a broken leg and hand. Raymond Waddell underwent surgery, but subsequently died of his injuries.

Some cross-conversion training took place through July and August with two Dakota captains receiving training in the two-seat Meteor. Flight Lieutenant Warwick Addison AFC, who had flown Bristol Beaufighters in the Second World War, subsequently went solo in the single-seat Meteor. In September, one of the two-seat Meteors was lost in bad weather, killing the pilot, Sergeant Al Avery, and his passenger, Flight Lieutenant Henry Johnston. Squadron Leader Murdoch overflew the area the next day, searching for the missing pilot; Avery's body washed ashore at Aomi-Shima Island while Murdoch was airborne.

This Dakota bears the badge of No 36 Squadron on its nose following the changeover
from No 30 Transport Unit in March 1953. (Australian War Memorial)

No 30 Transport Unit undertook a special flight on the seventh anniversary of the dropping
of the atomic bomb on 6 August 1945 when Flight Lieutenant James Lynch flew a Dakota
over Hiroshima to drop a wreath in remembrance of the victims.

Late in the year, the demand for VIP transport flights increased, including the task of
conveying the Minister for Navy and Air, William McMahon. The time had also arrived
for Murdoch to pass command to Squadron Leader Malcolm Humphrey DFC. The new
commanding officer had distinguished himself during the Second World War with No 455
Squadron RAAF when, flying a Handley Page Hampden, he was wounded in both legs
while conducting a torpedo attack on shipping.

On Christmas Eve 1952, the number of medical evacuees carried by the unit passed 10,000
and, the next day, Humphrey flew the only Christmas Day sortie, a traditional Freight
Special, delivering mail and freight to Seoul.

February 1953 farewelled Lieutenant General Bridgeford as Commander-in-Chief of the
British Commonwealth Forces in Korea and No 30 Transport Unit marked the departure
of their long-term VIP passenger by dispatching a Dakota to escort his Qantas Skymaster as
it departed Japan. His replacement, Lieutenant General Henry Wells, immediately utilised
the Australian Dakotas, frequently flying between Tokyo and Seoul for reasons that soon
became evident.

Having been reformed as No 36 Squadron on 9 March, the unit flew the first prisoner
exchange flight from Seoul to Japan, consisting of six stretcher-bound and 12 walking
former prisoners of war (POW). Lieutenant General Wells met the first arrivals in person.
This was the beginning of Operation *Little Switch* across the United Nations Command that
saw sick and wounded prisoners repatriated and offered some hope the conflict was drawing
to a close. However, within days, multiple 'Rocket Specials' were also flown to Kimpo.

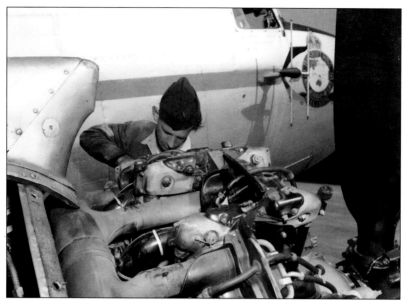

Iwakuni, Japan. 1952. Corporal K. Sumner, RAAF engine fitter, works on the starboard engine of a Douglas C47 Dakota aircraft of no. 30 communications unit.

The hours accumulated as the crossings of the Sea of Japan continued to carry the supplies of the war, freight, personnel and medical evacuees. Wells continued to fly almost daily in the Dakota designated for VIP transport, A65-114. The commitment did not abate until the Armistice agreement was signed on 27 July 1953 when a return freighter and courier flight were flown to Seoul and the Canadian ambassador was conveyed to Tokyo. The war had ended; the transport flight that had morphed into No 36 Squadron had flown more than 700 hours for the month.

In April, *Little Switch* had sought to exchange and repatriate limited numbers of sick and wounded prisoners of war. With the Armistice came Operation *Big Switch*. August 1953 called for the squadron to fly 'POW Specials' as part of the broader program to repatriate all prisoners of war. Throughout the month, three flights each day would transport the former prisoners to Japan.

The squadron remained in Japan until it returned to Australia in March 1955. A continued presence was maintained at Iwakuni until September 1956 in the form of RAAF Transport Flight (Japan), operating three Dakotas and a single Wirraway. However, beyond the length of service, the statistics surrounding the RAAF transport operation during the Korean War speak most loudly.

Conducted day and night in an environment of extreme weather, inhospitable terrain, minimal aids to navigation, and at times subject to enemy fire, the flight crews and supporting ground personnel provided a dependable lifeline to the battlefield and beyond. When the Armistice was signed, the transport unit that had become No 36 Squadron had carried more than 100,000 personnel, more than 6,000 tonnes of freight and, crucially, undertaken nearly 13,000 medical evacuations.

Chapter 18
NURSING AND MEDEVAC

Australian military nurses had been a part of the battlefield's landscape since the first of their number set sail from the colonies to serve in the Boer War in 1899. The subsequent century saw rapid advances in the management of combat casualties, the Korean War providing a notable landmark with the advent of mobile surgical units close to the front line and the evacuation of the wounded by helicopter. The Royal Australian Air Force Nursing Service (RAAFNS) was integral to the evolution of medical evacuations that took place during the conflict.

The RAAFNS was not a newcomer to medical evacuations, or medevacs, with specialised teams performing the role in the Second World War. These teams were part of the RAAF Medical Air Evacuation Transport Unit (MAETU), the first of which came into being in 1944 and the second in 1945. Only a limited number of nurses were selected from the RAAFNS and were specially trained for in-flight medical care and tropical hygiene. Deployed to Morotai and New Guinea, they provided a chain of evacuation from the South-West Pacific Theatre to hospitals in Australia. Even so, by war's end, less than 50 flight nurses had been trained to operate with the MAETU and the unit was disbanded soon after, having repatriated prisoners of war to Australia.

Post-war, the RAAFNS transitioned to train all nursing recruits in aeromedical evacuation, rather than the elite teams that characterised the MAETUs of the Second World War. All RAAFNS trainees now received training in aviation medicine, a demonstration of air-sea rescue, participated in a dinghy drill, and undertook training flights aboard various aircraft.

The evolution of medical air evacuations during the Korean War saw the introduction of the helicopter and the employment of US Mobile Army Surgical Hospital (MASH) units, the latter having been founded towards the close of the Second World War. However, the helicopters were limited by their capacity to carry only two stretcher cases in daylight hours, with further limitations imposed by the weather. Consequently, as part of the United Nations (UN) forces, only about 4% of casualties were airlifted by helicopter. Still, the challenging terrain of the Korean landscape meant that, for some, an evacuation by helicopter was the only option.

For the majority, stretcher bearers remained the primary means of initial conveyance to an aid post and from there they would be transferred by field ambulance to a clearing station, or a MASH unit. In time, Commonwealth MASH units were established, based on the US model. It was here that casualties would first encounter the Australian nurses of the RAAFNS who would prepare them for aerial evacuation to medical facilities in Japan.

A USAF Sikorsky H-5 taking a patient on board for evacuation. (Ces Sly)

The task of flying the wounded to Japan fell to the Australian Dakotas. At the outset of the Korean conflict, the RAAF had only three aircraft available and these were in high demand. This meant the evacuation of Australian casualties to Japan was initially accommodated in limited numbers aboard American aircraft. The shortfall of aircraft was overcome in November 1950 when a further four C-47s arrived from Malaya where they had been in service with No 38 Squadron during the Malayan Emergency. The Dakota could be configured to carry 24 stretcher patients or 27 ambulatory patients. However, more routinely, it was a combination of patients, five on litters and 20 'walking wounded' that would set course from Kimpo, Yeongdeungpo, Pyeongtaek or Pusan.

Six nursing sisters were attached to the RAAF hospital at Iwakuni, Japan, to conduct medical evacuations from Korea. At Iwakuni, they fed incoming patients and attended to their dressings and medication before they were transferred by train to the British Commonwealth General Hospital in Kure under the care of Australian Army nurses. Sister Patricia Furbank recalled the transport of the wounded when interviewed for the Australians at War Film Archive in March 2004:

> Well the Americans, they were en masse really. There were so many more than our troops, very bad injuries, much the same I guess as ours but in much larger numbers. They had a lot of paraplegics.
>
> That was another way we used to nurse them too. The same injuries but in a much larger number. Unfortunately, we did carry a lot of boys that had been addicted to morphine and that was hard because you knew they were in pain but you couldn't give them morphine anyway.

Typically, nursing sisters of the RAAFNS at Iwakuni would begin their day predawn, preparing to fly to K14 Kimpo, today the site of Gimpo International Airport. Kimpo was located near Seoul, hosted both United States and UN units and was reached by a four-hour flight across the Sea of Japan. Each nursing sister carried food and drink for the flight, in addition to a drug box that contained morphine, among other items; this was a responsibility taken seriously by the RAAFNS nurses.

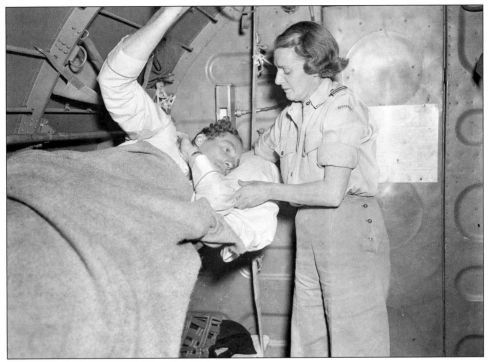

RAAF Nursing Sister Lou Marshall preparing a casualty for an evacuation flight from Yeongdeungpo airfield, South Korea, to Japan in 1951. (Australian War Memorial)

The patients would arrive by road from MASH units before they were assessed at Kimpo by a doctor and an RAAFNS nursing sister as to their suitability for air transport. With no doctor on board, the flight nurse would be solely responsible for the patient's welfare in flight and consequently had the final say on a patient's suitability to travel by air. Originally, the wounded were assessed in a hut, not far from the edge of the runway, but by 1952 a dedicated staging station had been established in Seoul which was staffed by an RAAFNS nursing sister on a rotational basis.

Before flight, the nursing sister would supervise the loading of the patients and complete the associated manifests and paperwork before briefing the pilot regarding those on board and any special requirements. As the Dakota's cabin was neither lined nor pressurised, the environment was both noisy and subjected to the sub-zero chill of the Korean winter. This was evident from the moment the aircraft began their rattling ground run along the Pierced Steel Planking (PSP) runway before taking to the sky.

On board, the nursing sisters provided refreshments and endeavoured to make the patients as comfortable as possible. The limitations of the C-47 meant it was unable to climb above much of the prevailing weather, making for a freezing trip in the winter months and a turbulent ride among the billowing clouds of the equally severe summer. Attempts to climb too high above the weather could potentially lead to a lack of oxygen, or hypoxia, affecting both the patients and the escorting nurses. In the winter, the aircraft were also at the mercy of the elements externally with airframe icing a challenge.

Having recovered, yet not sufficiently to return to their units in the field, patients returned to Australia on chartered Qantas flights, escorted by an RAAFNS nursing sister. Initially, these flights flew via the Philippines, but the route later changed to transit Guam and Port Moresby. The journey was without overnight stops, only staying for a few hours at each port of call to refuel before completing the flight, with up to 30 hours spent in the air. In total, RAAFNS sisters accompanied 728 patients on their flights home.

Recently released prisoner of war, Flight Lieutenant John 'Butch' Hannan chats with RAAF Nursing Sister Helen Blair in the back of a Dakota of No 36 Squadron. Fellow former prisoner, Pilot Officer Vance Drummond, is seated far left. (Australian War Memorial)

The Australian Korean War Nominal Roll lists 21 RAAFNS personnel serving during the Korean War. The nursing sisters involved in the medical air evacuations witnessed injuries sustained at the hands of the enemy and the elements. Exposed to bitter winters and extreme heat in the summer, the harsh environment inflicted a substantial toll upon troops. Frostbite and small-arms fire were equally as dangerous to those serving in the Korean War.

From a broader perspective, the Korean War consolidated the value of aircraft in the execution of medical care for the wounded. Airlifting a patient from the environs of the battlefield and evacuating them to hospital care in Japan saw the wounded receiving initial triage and clinical care beyond basic first aid far more quickly than in previous conflicts. This translated into better health outcomes and lower mortality rates. At 2.5%, the mortality rate of Australian troops that reached a forward medical facility was far lower than in preceding conflicts.

Those that served with the RAAFNS oversaw more than 12,700 personnel evacuated from Korea to Japan between January 1951 and December 1953, with the Armistice having been signed earlier on 27 July. Their contribution was vital to those wounded in the field and to the advancement of medical air evacuations.

Chapter 19
BEHIND ENEMY LINES

Abandoning an aircraft is the final option for a pilot. It can be a decision made in an instant, or as a final act after limping a damaged machine towards the nearest means of rescue. During the Korean War, leaving the aircraft was a challenging exercise in itself and the options on the ground were potentially even more dire. Those who parachuted to earth were known to be fired upon as they slowly approached the ground and, once there, were faced with potentially evading the enemy, being captured, or killed engaging the enemy.

Survival equipment was limited as it all had to be worn by the pilot so as to remain with him when he left the aircraft. It included a life jacket, emergency rations, a silk map, a first aid kit, a knife and a compass. The Americans were also issued with a radio set that not only allowed the downed pilot to communicate but transmitted a signal that rescuers could home in on. A small 'pointy talkie' book outlined basic phrases in Korean accompanied by the phonetic pronunciation printed in English.

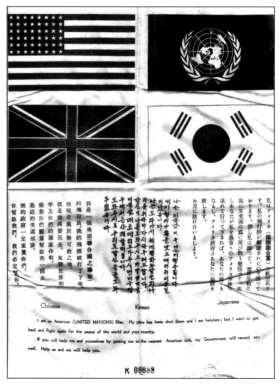

Blood Chit. Carried by aircrew, this cloth message conveyed a request for assistance to return their unit. (Owen Zupp)

Additionally, pilots possessed a blood chit. Measuring 20cm by 30cm, the white fabric rectangle was topped with the flags of the United States, the United Nations, Great Britain and the Republic of Korea. Beneath the flags, expressed in Chinese, Korean, Japanese and English, the blood chit read:

> I am an American (UNITED NATIONS) flier. My plane has been shot down and I am helpless, but I want to get back and fight again for the peace of the world and your country. If you will help me and yourselves by getting me to the nearest American unit, my Government will reward you well. Help us and we will help you.

At the bottom, an alphanumeric code could be traced to the owner of the chit.

The first step for a pilot in peril remained to get clear of the aircraft and, for many, there was minimal training in baling out. A single page of 12 paragraphs within the pilot's notes for the Mustang outlined the procedure of jettisoning the canopy, exiting the cockpit and operating the parachute. Raising the seat, trimming the aircraft, disconnecting the headphones, or, if at high altitude, changing the setting on the oxygen-flow lever and taking deep breaths, or even holding one's breath, are just some of the points a pilot under pressure had to recall.

Having reported that he had been hit by flak and his engine's oil pressure was falling to zero, Sergeant Harold Strange was seen baling out on 19 March 1951. Two objects were seen to leave the cockpit, but no parachute was seen to open. It was assumed Strange had not correctly secured his parachute.

A day later, Sergeant Ces Sly was the centre of a dramatic helicopter rescue, having been forced to leave his aircraft at 1,500 feet when his cockpit filled with smoke and his Mustang streamed a trail of coolant after being hit by ground fire. Having opened the canopy to clear the smoke, Sly forgot to jettison it with the result his parachute pack caught on the canopy's edge as he sought to abandon the aircraft. Freeing himself, he tumbled from the wing in a somersaulting motion, striking the tail as it passed, before pulling the ripcord and floating down under fire from enemy troops below.

Parachuting from an aircraft was not straightforward and there were instances where the pilot chose to stay with the aircraft and make a forced landing. This was the option chosen by Pilot 3 Bill Harrop on 3 September 1950 when his Mustang ran low on fuel. Harrop survived the forced landing and signalled the circling Mustangs overhead that he was safely down, but the delay in a helicopter rescue proved fatal.

When No 77 Squadron moved from the Mustang to the Meteor, the many tactical advantages the age of jet fighters delivered invariably raised new challenges. Not the least of these challenges was how to facilitate the escape of a pilot from a doomed jet aircraft. The potential of near-supersonic airflow and aerodynamic G-forces of the new era of fighters compounded an already complex problem. The days of sliding back the canopy, stepping onto the wing and jumping were no longer feasible. Instead of jumping, the pilot needed to be ejected from the aircraft.

An artist's impression of the ejection of Warrant Officer Ron Guthrie from Meteor A77-721 on 29 August 1951.
(Artwork by Dennis Newton)

The concept of an ejection seat was not new, although significant development occurred during the Second World War. Post-war, the Martin-Baker company in England led the development of the concept, although its early ejection seats required the pilot to undo the harness to get away from the seat and then pull the parachute's ripcord. It was this early generation Martin-Baker ejection seat that was fitted to the Meteors and would be used in the skies over Korea.

Warrant Officer Ron Guthrie in A77-721 before being shot down and taken prisoner on 29 August 1951.
(Australian War Memorial)

While there had been an inadvertent ejection from a Meteor in June 1951, the first intentional ejection from an RAAF aircraft took place on 29 August 1951 over North Korea when Warrant Officer Ron Guthrie ejected after his aircraft had been crippled by cannon fire from a MiG-15. The encounter had thrown Guthrie's Meteor into a series of rolling manoeuvres and he realised he needed to abandon the aircraft. He jettisoned the canopy before reaching for the looped handle above his head which would both draw down a protective blind over his face and fire the cartridges that would blast his seat upwards along a pair of rails and clear of the aircraft.

With both hands, he pulled the handle down twice without success before he realised that, on one side of his chest, his pistol's holster was limiting his downward thrust while a first aid pouch was the obstruction on the other side. On the third attempt, the blind came down and the seat erupted beneath him. A moment later, he was unconscious. Guthrie had ejected at a speed of Mach 0.75 and an altitude of 39,000 feet, or nearly 12 kilometres above the earth, the highest recorded ejection at the time.

When consciousness returned, Guthrie drew his goggles up to his eyes and refitted his oxygen mask, both of which had been forced askew. Considering his options, rather than plummeting vertically, deploying his parachute early could make him drift towards friendly troops below (it did not). With this in mind, Guthrie released the ejection seat harness and kicked it away beneath its small drogue chute. He then pulled his ripcord and, with a sudden jerk, his parachute's canopy blossomed above him.

When No 77 Squadron moved to ground-attack operations in late 1951, the ability to eject was directly affected. The very manual process of ejection using the early generation of ejection seats called for adequate time to get clear of the aircraft and perform the necessary actions. This time equated to a minimum altitude that allowed the process to occur and for the parachute canopy to open, capture the air and facilitate a safe descent. While modern, more powerful ejection seats are designed to safely operate at zero altitude and zero forward speed, this was not the case with the early Martin-Baker.

Based upon known cases, it was later estimated that a minimum safe state of flight for ejection would be a minimum of 1,000 feet above the ground and flying with a climbing trajectory. This precluded a significant portion of ground-attack operations when strafing routinely took place below 100 feet and rockets were released at around 1,500 feet in a 35-degree dive towards the target.

Although a minimum altitude for ejection was not published, the pilots were anecdotally aware of the limitations of the Martin-Baker Mk.1. This was reflected on 15 June 1953 when Sergeant Donald Pinkstone ejected, having chosen to release the ejection seat harness before leaving from his stricken Meteor in order to minimise the time for deployment of his parachute. Conversely, when Flight Lieutenant Ian Purssey ejected at approximately 600 feet over the Taedong River estuary, it was witnessed by Sergeant Ken Towner who stated he had not seen Purssey separate from his seat.

Leading Aircraftman W Ferguson replacing a Meteor's explosive ejection-seat charge. (Australian War Memorial)

Having survived a descent beneath a silken canopy, pilots met with differing fates. The body of Bill Harrop, who had forced landed his aircraft due to fuel exhaustion, was located by Air Force Chaplain Squadron Leader Esmond New some months later. Local villagers related that his body was found in a field along with the bodies of two North Korean soldiers, the apparent aftermath of a lethal exchange.

Ces Sly spent more than an hour surrounded by enemy troops before he was airlifted to safety by a second rescue helicopter, the first having been repelled by fierce ground fire.

It took Ron Guthrie nearly half an hour to descend and, despite his best intentions, he would not escape the North Koreans below. Like Sly, he was fired upon in the final minutes of his descent and captured shortly after the epic journey earthward ended. Guthrie was incarcerated until his release in 1953.

Then there were those who came down behind enemy lines whose ultimate fates remain uncertain, or who to this day remain in their cockpits somewhere in the harsh landscape of North Korea.

Chapter 20
PRISONERS OF WAR

By the end of the Korean War, No 77 Squadron had seen seven of its pilots survive their various combat experiences to be taken into captivity as prisoners of war. Their treatment at the hands of their communist captors was brutal, being told they were not prisoners of war, but war criminals. This false categorisation supposedly allowed the Geneva Convention, to which China was a signatory, to be disregarded.

The intent of their captors extended beyond interrogation and intelligence gathering to indoctrination with the communist philosophy. Prisoners would be sent to be 'educated' through long sessions in the morning and afternoon. Reading literature was made available in the form of English-language communist newspapers from the west.

The other aspect of confinement, other than when temptations were being offered during interrogation and indoctrination, was inhuman punishment, abhorrent living conditions and a scarcity of food. Flight Lieutenant Gordon Harvey, the first No 77 Squadron prisoner of war, was released in 1953, losing 20 kilograms and having developed a stutter during his incarceration.

The RAAF was aware of the methods employed against prisoners by the Communists and produced a document titled 'Interrogation and Security Brief for Korea – Including Communistic Indoctrination.'

The comprehensive briefing reminded downed airmen the war was not over for them but had changed to a psychological battle with the enemy. It spoke of the various ploys of interrogation that would be employed at the various early stages of their confinement. It warned they would be moved about in the initial stages and interrogated frequently until their final incarceration at a camp. It was here the indoctrination would take place. Letter writing would be withheld to lower morale and under no circumstances should prisoners agree to participate in broadcasts or offer a signature that could be copied and misrepresented. Even though the prison camp might seem like the final destination, airmen were cautioned that the 'interrogation never ends'. Despite the thoroughness and detail contained within the briefing, it did not refer to the cages or darkened holes in which the prisoners could be confined. Nor did it mention 'Pak's Palace' where the commandant, Major Pak, handed out sadistic treatment.

Exiting his Mustang, Gordon Harvey had started to make his way towards a building across the frozen river when bullets began to throw up chips of ice. Surrendering to his pursuers, he was walked from house to house where he was abused by the local population. Over the next three months, Harvey was moved about and frequently, brutally, interrogated, including during a term at 'Pak's Palace'. At one time he was interviewed by the Western journalist and conspirator, William Burchett. Knowing of Burchett's communist leanings, Harvey was guarded and made no complaints, aware they may leak back to his captors. Burchett did ask Harvey how he had been treated and the journalist was taken aback when the pilot replied, with understatement, 'Very badly'.

Forced into labour near P'yŏngyang, Harvey was tasked with carrying water over long distances and clearing out the raw sewage spilling from toilets. By night, he dug revetments to conceal vehicles, conveyed supplies and was witness to the American B-26s flying night bombing missions, almost becoming a casualty. The food and accommodation were disgusting and the working hours long.

In April 1951, Harvey escaped with two other prisoners and was on the run for six days. Heading to the coast, they attempted to steal a boat and proceed to the UN-occupied island of Ch'odo but were unsuccessful and were captured a few days later further south, near Sariwon, 60 miles (96 kilometres) from 'Pak's Palace'. All the escapees were severely punished and beaten with Harvey spending nearly a month in 'The Hole'. Dug into the side of a hill, the dark cavity was two metres deep and one-metre square.

A propaganda photograph showing POWs eating apples in the Other Ranks POW camp at Pyŏktong during the winter of 1952–53 when the temperature dropped as low as minus-43 degrees Celsius. The photo was taken by a Chinese interpreter. Ron Guthrie, seated centre, stole the photo from the interpreter's desk. (Australian War Memorial)

Ron Guthrie suffered similar treatment following his record ejection from Meteor A77-721 on 29 August 1951. Like Harvey, Guthrie was paraded before abusive citizens following his capture. He was then stripped to his underwear and forced into a makeshift cage constructed from a packing case. His next confinement was in a dark, wet dungeon and, on another occasion, he was strapped to a chair in the town square and children were encouraged to torment, poke and spit at him. Guthrie was also a 'guest' at 'Pak's Palace'.

He was interrogated by two Europeans, one of whom was Russian and a pilot who held the Meteor in low regard but respected the F-86 Sabre as one had shot him down. He was also interrogated at the MiG-15s' home at Antung by two women who excitedly wrote down notes when he told them of the Meteor's aft-firing cannon. When the false 'intelligence' reached more knowledgeable ears, Ron was punished for his insubordination. Guthrie also affected an escape with two other prisoners and hoped to take a boat to Ch'odo but was also recaptured. He was brutally marched north to the camp at Pinchong Ni where he met Gordon Harvey.

Sergeant Vance Drummond survived 45 minutes on the ground after ejecting from his Meteor following the dog fight of 1 December 1951. His tracks in the snow led the North Korean soldiers to his location and his incarceration began, along with Sergeant Bruce Thomson who had been shot down in the same air battle. The two pilots joined Harvey and Guthrie at the camp at Pinchong Ni and also escaped for a short period of freedom in April 1952 before being recaptured.

Flight Lieutenant John 'Butch' Hannan was the fifth pilot to be taken prisoner near Sibyon-Ni after ejecting from his burning Meteor on 6 February 1952. The next to be captured was Flight Lieutenant Olaf Bergh (Royal Air Force) whose starboard engine and cockpit had been struck by ground fire before the engine suddenly exploded. Ejecting at low level, he landed seconds after his parachute had slowed his descent. With Meteors and then American F-4U Corsairs roaring overhead in his defence, Bergh sought to evade his captors who were randomly firing into nearby bushes. At one point he raised his arm to wave his Mae West life vest as a signal to the aircraft overhead, only to have the vest immediately punctured by two bullets.

He drank from paddy fields and kept moving until the fifth night when he walked straight into a Chinese sentry and was taken prisoner. Bergh was interrogated over three months and was told that, as a war criminal, he had no rights. He subsequently spent two months in solitary confinement at 'Pak's Palace'.

On 15 June 1953, the final No 77 Squadron pilot to be taken prisoner was Sergeant Donald Pinkstone when his Meteor was hit by flak and set alight. A rescue helicopter sent to rescue him was repelled by enemy fire and he was captured and imprisoned with the Armistice a little more than a month away.

Those pilots already captive were first allowed to write letters and then saw a slight improvement in their food which indicated peace might be approaching. It was still some time coming as the issue of prisoners continued to stall negotiations.

Panmunjom, North Korea, 29 August 1953. After two-and-a-half years in captivity, Flight Lieutenant Gordon Harvey (without hat) is escorted to freedom by, left to right, Squadron Leader Neville McNamara (Executive Officer, No 77 Squadron), Wing Commander Alan Hodges (Commanding Officer, No 77 Squadron) and Ms Phil Daymon (Australian Red Cross representative). (Australian War Memorial)

While the Australians were keen to return home, not all the captured North Koreans wished to be repatriated. The UN insisted repatriation be voluntary but, until the final months of the war, the Communists insisted all prisoners be returned regardless of their will.

The first weakening of the policy came with the agreement to exchange and repatriate sick and wounded prisoners in April 1953 under Operation *Little Switch*. Full agreement on voluntary repatriation was significant in the signing of the Armistice on 27 July 1953. Operation *Big Switch*, to repatriate all prisoners of war, commenced on 5 August with No 36 Squadron Dakotas flying numerous 'Prisoner Specials' between Korea and Japan.

The first pilot to be taken prisoner, Gordon Harvey, spent more than three and a half years in captivity. The final No 77 Squadron pilot to return was Donald Pinkstone on 5 September 1953. All seven airmen returned from an environment where at least 13,000 UN prisoners had died in captivity.

Former POWs returning from North Korea. The man with the yellow scarf is Ron Guthrie. (Australian War Memorial)

Ex-prisoners of war about to board a Qantas aircraft prior to leaving Japan for Australia. Left to right: Flight Lieutenant Gordon Harvey, Flying Officer Bruce Thomson, Sergeant Donald Pinkstone, Flying Officer Vance Drummond, and Flight Lieutenants John Hannan and Ron Guthrie. (Australian War Memorial)

Chapter 21
BEYOND THE PARALLEL

The outbreak of the Korean War on 25 June 1950 placed the Royal Australian Air Force (RAAF) firmly in the frame for the opening volleys in both operational and political spheres. Circumstances had evolved that positioned both the Australian Government and its RAAF Mustang fighter squadron in Japan as central players in the conflict on the Korean Peninsula.

In its British Commonwealth Occupation Force service, No 77 Squadron had remained an active and highly valued member of the forces in Japan. A number of its pilots were experienced Second World War veterans and the Mustangs were continually flown on gunnery, rocketry and bombing training sorties, in addition to competitions with the United States Air Force (USAF). Highly trained, in Japan and conversant with the USAF's structure, No 77 Squadron was well positioned to participate in action on the Korean Peninsula, albeit with their aircraft having been readied for the looming voyage home.

The squadron had already established a respected reputation with General Stratemeyer and the Far East Air Force (FEAF) and, importantly, it was the only available operational Mustang squadron. The USAF had entered the jet age and local units were equipped with F-80 Shooting Stars; these lacked the endurance to participate in the bomber escort and ground-attack missions that characterised the beginning of the war.

The first meeting of Australia, New Zealand and United States (ANZUS) representatives at Pearl Harbor in 1952. Seated from left: Lieutenant General SF Rowell (Australian Chief of General Staff), Admiral AW Radford (US Commander-in-Chief, Pacific), and Major General WG Gentry (New Zealand Chief of General Staff). (Australian War Memorial)

It was late July 1950 before the first USAF F-51 Mustangs arrived, on board the Essex-class aircraft carrier USS *Boxer*, and even longer before Air National Guard Mustang units were combat ready to deploy to Korea. Consequently, No 77 Squadron's immediate involvement was welcomed by the FEAF and contributed to building the relationship between Australia and the United States on an even larger scale.

Politically, Mr PC 'Percy' Spender, the Australian External Affairs Minister, had eyed the North Atlantic Treaty with interest since it was signed in 1949. The treaty was the legal basis upon which the North Atlantic Treaty Organisation (NATO) was founded and created a formal military alliance between the United States and Western European nations as the Cold War emerged.

Spender believed the need for such an agreement between Pacific nations and the United States existed, as Australia's military experience in the Pacific during the Second World War had shown. In March 1950, Spender had addressed parliament regarding the potential of a 'Pacific Pact', highlighting that he had, '… in mind particularly the United States of America, whose participation would give such a pact a substance that it would otherwise lack.'

The outbreak of war in Korea and the immediate involvement of the Australian Mustangs could be seen as evidence of Australia's commitment and was apparent when Spender met President Truman on 1 September to discuss the possibility of such a pact. Only weeks after the war had started, Spender reassured the president that Australia, '… could be counted upon in any emergency to give the utmost of her manpower and equipment to meet all new crises.'

The discussions continued and, in a telegram on 28 May 1951, President Truman replied in kind to Prime Minister Menzies stating, '… I can assure you that we are fully mindful and appreciative of the fine contribution which Australia has made in Korea from the very beginning of hostilities.' Ultimately, the Pacific Pact came to be known as the Australia, New Zealand and United States Security Treaty, or ANZUS Treaty, and was signed on 1 September 1951. It is a treaty that has survived to the present day and whose origins lay in part with the immediate involvement of the RAAF at the outbreak of the Korean War.

Chapter 22
IN REVIEW

From the first days of the war when the Mustangs escorted USAF B-29 Superfortress bombers and flew ground-attack missions, to the day of the Armistice when RAAF Meteor F.8 jet fighters flew rocket strikes and armed-reconnaissance missions, No 77 Squadron changed roles a number of times, just as the use of air power varied.

Initially, air power sought to destroy the enemy's capacity to conduct war through precision bombing which saw the squadron escorting those missions. With the rapid advance southward by North Korean forces, the squadron's role evolved into close support of ground troops defending the Pusan Perimeter and flying interdiction missions in an attempt to disrupt the enemy's stretched supply lines.

Pilot 2 (P2) James Hilary 'Jim' Flemming standing on the wing of a No 77 Squadron Mustang (A68-757). Flemming would rise to the rank of air-vice marshal. (Australian War Memorial)

Following the Inch'ŏn landing and the breakout at Pusan, the Australian Mustangs supported the UN forces moving north to the Yalu River where the MiG-15 emerged and removed the previously unchallenged air superiority of the allies. With the entry of the Chinese into the

164

war at the close of 1950, the UN forces again moved south, this time to the 38th Parallel where close-support missions covered the movement. Coincident with No 77 Squadron re-equipping with the Gloster Meteor in mid-1951, the Korean War entered a stalemate that would remain until the Armistice and, after a period of flying fighter sweeps, the squadron was relegated to an air-defence role before finding its final purpose in ground attack.

This continual shift in roles highlighted the need for the squadron to be flexible and adaptive. Its tasking on armed reconnaissances would see the Mustangs loaded with a combination of .50-calibre rounds, napalm, bombs or rockets. Specific targets were not briefed before a flight but would see the Mustangs directed to targets once airborne with the USAF *Mosquito* forward air control aircraft selecting targets. Even then, the target could be changed mid-flight.

The interdiction and bombing campaign that accompanied the stalemate from mid-1951 proved costly to the UN forces and it was evident the North Koreans and Chinese were adept and repairing much of the damage quickly. United States Lieutenant General Otto P Weyland proposed the strategy should incur 'the maximum amount of selected destruction, thus making the Korean Conflict as costly as possible to the enemy in terms of equipment, supplies, and personnel', a strategy that would hopefully also prove costly to the Chinese and Russians supplying the war. With the arrival of General Mark Clark, this strategy, known as 'Air Pressure', was adopted in May 1952 and the Meteors played their role in attacking power stations and substantial infrastructure.

The selection of the Gloster Meteor F.8 as the replacement jet fighter for the RAAF during the Korean War stemmed from the United States' production of the F-86 Sabre straining to supply the USAF, without being able to provide the aircraft to Allied air forces. The South African Air Force opted for the Sabre, but it was February 1953 before their first Sabres arrived, only a matter of months before the Armistice.

The deployment of the Meteor as an interceptor to engage the MiG-15 in fighter sweeps and its subsequent withdrawal from the role is central to many discussions regarding No 77 Squadron's involvement in the Korean jet war. Early trials suggested the Meteor was competitive with the MiG below 20,000 feet, where it could utilise its acceleration and sustained rate of turn, yet its early fighter sweeps were flown above 30,000 feet as top cover for the USAF Sabres. Furthermore, it has been considered the Meteor may have continued in the role if deployed at the lower altitudes, such as the missions where it covered bombing missions by USAF B-26 Invaders.

The record shows the Meteors did not fare particularly well in air-to-air combat against the MiG-15, despite the blurred claims and counter-claims of victories that saw both sides close to parity. Pilot Officer, later Air Vice-Marshal, Bill Simmonds, who achieved an aerial victory over the MiG-15, highlighted that specific air-combat tactics were needed to suit the Meteor:

> So it was a pretty formidable platform at those heights. The unfortunate thing is that we hadn't developed the tactics to exploit that aircraft at the altitudes that we should

have been flying it at. And it wasn't until, you know, many years later that there was a realisation that air combat tactics was almost a science and that we had to develop our own tactics for a particular set of circumstances.

The MiG-15 did not have to dogfight and expose itself to unnecessary risk but could use its superior height and speed to hit and run, as Allied aircraft had done in the Second World War, rather than tangle with the more manoeuvrable Mitsubishi A6M 'Zero' in a twisting, turning, slower fight. Pilot Officer 'Jake' Newham, who rose to the rank of air marshal and the position of Chief of the Air Staff, also raised a valid argument, stating, 'The fact is, you don't do air fighting by sucking people into your 6 o'clock and that's the only place you are going to get MiGs …' The adage of having the advantage of altitude and speed dated back to the days of the Red Baron and the First World War and remained valid at the dawn of the jet age.

Flight Lieutenant Neville Patrick McNamara, No 82 (Fighter) Squadron, British Commonwealth Occupation Force, rose to dizzying heights in the RAAF, becoming Air Marshal Sir Neville Patrick McNamara after service as Chief of the Air Staff, RAAF, and Chief of the Defence Force Staff. (Australian War Memorial)

Newham was just one of the pilots who saw service in Korea and subsequently went on to senior roles within the RAAF. Eventual Air Chief Marshal Sir Neville McNamara KBE AO AFC AE also rose to become Chief of the Air Staff and, in turn, Chief of the Defence Force Staff. Exchange pilot Flight Lieutenant Keith Williamson would complete his career as Marshal of the Royal Air Force Sir Keith Williamson GCB AFC. A further seven No 77 Squadron pilots would rise to the rank of air vice-marshal, while Flight Lieutenant David Hitchins of No 30 Transport Unit would retire with the rank of air commodore.

Flight Lieutenant Keith Williamson (RAF) climbs aboard his Meteor. The English exchange pilot would become Marshal of the Royal Air Force Sir Keith Alec Williamson GCB AFC. (Alan Royston)

The RAAF had lost a substantial number of experienced personnel in the demobilisation that followed the end of the Second World War; however, the Korean War provided a significant number of leaders who would see the RAAF through later decades. Additionally, these pilots had gathered valuable experience in combat operations at the dawn of the jet-fighter age.

In being the first RAAF jet fighter to see operational service, the Meteor performed admirably in the ground-attack role, although its vulnerable ventral tank was not well suited to such combat. Nor was the Meteor originally equipped with rocket rails and, even when fitted, experience modified the dive by which the rockets were delivered. Even so, No 77 Squadron went on to successfully employ rockets and even adapt them to deliver napalm. As much as the squadron's operational success was in the ground-attack role, the timeframe in which they pivoted and reorganised from flying air defence to ground attack was measured in weeks, which was a sterling effort under Wing Commander Ron Susans.

The tireless work of No 30 Transport Unit in both supplying and transporting troops was a critical role. The C-47 Dakotas often flew in hazardous conditions posed by both the environment and the enemy. The unit also provided a critical role in providing medical evacuations, evacuating more than 13,000 patients by the Armistice. Furthermore, the RAAF Nursing Service (RAAFNS) had evolved from providing a specialised group of nurses with aeromedical training to integrating the skillset into the training of all nurses of the RAAFNS.

The extremes of the Korean environment also provided hazardous conditions for those on the ground. From boiling summer heat to frozen winters, the ground crews of the maintenance units armed and maintained the aircraft around the clock. In addition to routine scheduled maintenance, there were unforeseen unserviceabilities and the inevitable battle damage that needed to be repaired. Susans reflected that the 1,000-mission month in February 1952 was only made possible by ground crews refuelling aircraft from drums day and night.

Perhaps the greatest legacy of the RAAF's involvement in the Korean War was the realisation that pilot training at the time did not adequately prepare new arrivals from Australia to enter the conflict. At the forefront of this shift in thinking was Squadron Leader Dick Cresswell. He had flown jet operations with the USAF in preparation for the conversion to the Meteor and became aware of the advanced training USAF pilots received, particularly in the area of instrument flying.

Under the leadership of Wing Commander Cresswell, the Fighter Combat Instructor Course was developed and remains in operation to this day. (via Owen Zupp)

Cresswell later commanded No 2 Operational Training Unit, which was reformed at RAAF Williamtown in March 1952, and continued to be developed as a means of providing advanced training for fighter pilots; it survives today as No 2 Operational Conversion Unit. Furthermore, Cresswell founded the Fighter Combat Instructor course in 1954 to provide specialised training for instructors tasked with training fighter pilots.

The Korean War provided many firsts. It will always be remembered as the first jet war, but it was also a limited war and indicative of future conflicts. For the RAAF, the Korean War reinvigorated the Service, drastically reduced in size following the post–Second World

War demobilisation, and schooled a new generation of future leaders. In working under the command of the USAF's Fifth Air Force, and in close cooperation with American squadrons, forward air controllers, ground troops and air traffic controllers, the Australians were active in joint-force cooperation and coordination.

A formation of de Havilland DH.100 Vampires from No 2 Operational Conversion Unit during a training flight out of RAAF Williamtown. (Australian War Memorial)

Involvement in the Korean War had been unforeseen to the extent the Mustangs of No 77 Squadron were already prepared for shipping home and its pilots celebrating their impending exit as the North Koreans initiated their advance south on 25 June 1950. Within days, the squadron was on a war footing and, on 2 July 1950, flew its first mission of nearly 19,000. It was a commitment that cost 42 lives, including two members of No 30 Transport Unit lost in accidents.

In some quarters, the Korean War has come to be known as the 'Forgotten War', however, it has not been forgotten by those who served and those who live on the Korean Peninsula. Equally, it should be remembered whenever the proudest traditions of the RAAF come to mind.

Chapter 23
THE FINAL MISSIONS

The honour roll at the Australian War Memorial in Canberra lists the names of those members of the Royal Australian Air Force (RAAF) that paid the ultimate sacrifice during their service in the Korean War. Serving alongside these men, four members of the Royal Air Force (RAF) also lost their lives in the skies over Korea.

Some are interred in the United Nations Memorial Cemetery at Busan, South Korea, and others in the Yokohama War Cemetery, Japan. However, for most of those that perished, there is no final resting place beyond the Korean soil where their aircraft met its end.

The United Nations Memorial Cemetery Korea in Busan, Republic of Korea, where the Wall of Remembrance lists the names of all who made the supreme sacrifice. (Defence)

Their final moments are recorded in the narratives of those pilots that returned from that mission – a few words describing a final radio transmission, the separation of a wing or impact with the ground. Even so, having not made their final journey home, they are listed as 'Missing in Action'.

Following are the brave men of the RAAF and RAF that rest in the land of the morning calm with no known grave.

Sergeant Donald Campbell Ellis

Date of Loss: 22 December 1950

Commemorated on Wall 1 of the Wall of Remembrance at the United Nations Memorial Cemetery – Busan, Korea

Sergeant Ellis was participating in an armed reconnaissance of the Taedong River, which flows north to south through the North Korean capital, Pyongyang. Flying North American P-51D Mustang, A68-726, in a formation of two aircraft along the city's perimeter at 200 feet, Ellis called that he was going to crash.

The pilot of the lead aircraft looked back to see Ellis's aircraft 'burning furiously' on the ground having disintegrated on impact. Having orbited overhead and seeing no sign of Ellis, his fellow pilot departed the crash site, encountering ground fire nearby.

Sergeant Don Ellis was posthumously promoted to the rank of Pilot Officer and awarded the United States Distinguished Flying Cross and Air Medal.

Sergeant Geoffrey Ingham Stephens

Date of Loss: 6 January 1951

Commemorated on Wall 2 of the Wall of Remembrance at the United Nations Memorial Cemetery – Busan, Korea

Sergeant Stephens was one of a pair of P-51D Mustangs tasked with an armed reconnaissance along the main road north of the South Korean capital, Seoul. Flying Mustang A68-765 at 100 feet in trail behind the other aircraft, the leader noticed a flash of flame. Turning back to investigate, a 30-metre charred track along the ground led to the burning wreck of Stephens' Mustang.

Stephens had been lost in the vicinity of the Imjin River in an area today that constitutes a portion of the demilitarised zone (DMZ). At the time of the loss, the territory had recently been overrun in a Chinese attack that pushed United Nations forces south across the Han River and out of Seoul.

Sergeant Geoffrey Stephens was posthumously promoted to the rank of Pilot Officer and awarded the United States Distinguished Flying Cross and Air Medal.

Sergeant Harold Thomas Strange

Date of Loss: 19 March 1951

Commemorated on Wall 2 of the Wall of Remembrance at the United Nations Memorial Cemetery – Busan, Korea

Sergeant Strange was flying as one of two Mustangs conducting a road reconnaissance to the west of Wonsan. The pilot of the leading aircraft would recount that there was a 'fair amount of flak' at one stage during the flight. Strange reported falling oil pressure in the engine of his P51D Mustang A68-782 and his leader responded by ordering him to turn east towards

Wonsan, where a United States Navy vessel was operating in the harbour and could dispatch a rescue helicopter.

Over the harbour at 1,500 feet, Strange was ordered to bail out. His canopy was jettisoned and then two dark objects were seen to leave the aircraft and fall into the sea without a parachute being sighted. It was speculated that Strange had become separated from his parachute.

Despite a substantial search until sunset, which included the US Navy vessel, fixed-wing aircraft and helicopters, no sign of Strange was found other than a few items related to his Mustang.

Sergeant Douglas Merson Robertson

Date of Loss: 11 November 1951

Commemorated on Wall 2 of the Wall of Remembrance at the United Nations Memorial Cemetery – Busan, Korea

Sergeant Robertson was one of twelve Gloster Meteor F.8 aircraft returning to their base at K14 Kimpo, having completed a combat air patrol (CAP). Flying Meteor A77-959 and using the callsign *Anzac Charlie 2*, Robertson was involved in a mid-air collision with another Meteor. While the other pilot was able to maintain control, although ultimately ejecting from his aircraft, Robertson was seen to immediately enter a steep spiral dive.

Two other Meteors followed the out-of-control aircraft down as it shed pieces, including its canopy, before ultimately impacting the ground. With the aircraft burning on the ground, no parachute was sighted by the other pilots who circled the area before their return to base.

Sergeant Douglas Robertson was posthumously promoted to the rank of Pilot Officer.

Sergeant Ernest Donald Armit

Date of Loss: 1 December 1951

Commemorated on Wall 1 of the Wall of Remembrance at the United Nations Memorial Cemetery – Busan, Korea

Sergeant Armit was flying Gloster Meteor F.8 A77-949 conducting a fighter sweep to the north of the North Korean capital, Pyongyang. Over Sunchon, the 12 Meteors were attacked by 20 MiG-15 aircraft, flown by Russian pilots of the 176th Guards Fighter Aviation Division (GIAD) and an air battle ensued.

From Australian and Russian records, the melee of the subsequent combat described Captain S.M. Kramarenko and his wingman attacking two Meteors on the outer right side of the formation, the element where Armit was stationed. As Kramarenko claimed hits all over his target, he noticed, '… the Meteor wingman's tail flying off as a result of a burst of fire from my wingman'. Interpreting accounts of the battle, this aircraft is thought to be that of Armit and one of two seen to be burning on the ground below – the other pilot having ejected.

Sergeant Don Armit was posthumously promoted to the rank of Pilot Officer and awarded the United States Air Medal.

Flight Lieutenant Mark Astil Baren Henry Aytack Browne-Gaylord DFC

Date of Loss: 27 January 1952

Commemorated on Wall 1 of the Wall of Remembrance at the United Nations Memorial Cemetery – Busan, Korea

Under the callsign *Black 2*, Flight Lieutenant Browne-Gaylord was flying Gloster Meteor F.8 A77-559 as one in a section of two aircraft conducting strafing attacks in the Chinnampo (N'ampo) area before setting course for K14 Kimpo under conditions of low cloud. With *Black 1* in the lead, the two aircraft encountered heavy ground fire north of Haeju, with Browne-Gaylord reporting the partial loss of his flight instruments, although he was not concerned.

Browne-Gaylord then called *Black 1* for a heading to fly to Kimpo, which he was given, but when *Black 1* called for a fuel check a few minutes later there was no response. *Black 1* turned back to search the area near Yonan but nothing was seen and no further radio transmissions were received.

Flight Lieutenant Harry Browne-Gaylord was posthumously awarded a Bar to the Distinguished Flying Cross.

Sergeant Bruce Thomson Gillan

Date of Loss: 27 January 1952

Commemorated on Wall 1 of the Wall of Remembrance at the United Nations Memorial Cemetery – Busan, Korea

Sergeant Gillan was flying Gloster Meteor F.8 A77-726 and having strafed Ongjin airfield flew west towards Haeju before commencing a pass on a water tower on the outskirts of Ch'wiya. Gillan then called that he'd been hit by ground fire and had a hole in the right wing. Flying at 600 feet in poor weather, Gillan called to the other Meteor of *Godfrey Black Section* that he was heading home.

The other Meteor, *Black 2*, called Gillan to say that his aircraft was streaming fuel but received no reply. The fuel stream then became a trail of smoke with pieces falling from the cockpit area. *Black 2* overtook Gillan's Meteor at 200 feet, noting that the canopy, the ejection seat and the pilot were not in the aircraft.

Black 2 turned back to search for Gillan but found nothing further. The next day searching Meteors located Gillan's aircraft in Haeju Bay on a mud bank, its rear section was distinguishable, but the rest of the aircraft had disintegrated on impact.

Sergeant Bruce Gillan was posthumously promoted to the rank of Pilot Officer and awarded the United States Air Medal.

Sergeant Richard George Robinson

Date of Loss: 16 February 1952

Commemorated on Wall 2 of the Wall of Remembrance at the United Nations Memorial Cemetery – Busan, Korea

Sergeant Robinson was flying Gloster Meteor F.8 A77-464 as one of four Meteors tasked to conduct a rocket strike, followed by an armed reconnaissance near Sariwon. West of Sinmak and at 200 feet, Robinson called, 'I'm hit and I'm getting out'.

Robinson's ventral tank was seen to be on fire and shortly afterwards the rear fuselage and tail separated from the aircraft and the Meteor crashed without the pilot being seen to eject. The Meteors then flew low over the main wreckage but there was no sign of life.

Sergeant Richard Robinson was posthumously promoted to the rank of Pilot Officer and awarded the United States Air Medal.

Sergeant Lionel Henry Cadogan Cowper

Date of Loss: 30 March 1952

Commemorated on Wall 1 of the Wall of Remembrance at the United Nations Memorial Cemetery – Busan, Korea

Sergeant Cowper was one of six Meteors on a rocket strike mission on buildings on the outskirts of Haeju. Flying Gloster Meteor F.8 A77-120, Cowper called that he was commencing his dive onto the target, a manoeuvre that commenced around 5,000 feet with rockets being released between 1,000 feet and 1,500 feet. A short time later smoke and flames consistent with an aircraft crash were observed in the target area.

From the after-action report, it was seen as unlikely that Cowper had fired his rockets and then he had failed to recover from the dive, suggesting that he had been struck by ground fire during the descent.

Sergeant Lionel Cowper was posthumously promoted to the rank of Pilot Officer and awarded the United States Air Medal.

Sergeant Maxwell Edwin Colebrook AM (US)

Date of Loss: 13 April 1952

Commemorated on Wall 1 of the Wall of Remembrance at the United Nations Memorial Cemetery – Busan, Korea

As one of two Gloster Meteor F.8 aircraft operating under the callsign of *Godfrey White*, Colebrook was participating in a patrol and armed reconnaissance of the main supply route (MSR) from Panmunjom to P'yŏngyang. Directed to a reported heavy gun position at Masan Ni, the pair of Meteors arrived overhead at 10,000 feet and identified the target.

The first aircraft dived and made a low pass on the target, followed by Colebrook in Meteor A77-627. As the first aircraft levelled at 5,000 feet, the pilot looked back to see dust clouds rising from the heavy gun position, consistent with it being strafed. Colebrook then called he had been hit and flashed past the other Meteor with the ventral tank of A77-627 on fire and was told to jettison the flaming fuel tank.

Seconds later Colebrook called that both engines were operating and he was heading home with his intentions relayed to the controlling agency at Kimpo by the other pilot. Despite several attempts to make contact, nothing further was heard from Colebrook and searches that day and the next found no trace of the pilot or his aircraft.

Sergeant Max Colebrook was posthumously promoted to the rank of Pilot Officer and awarded the Distinguished Flying Medal (DFM).

Flight Lieutenant Ian Goodwin Swan Purssey AM (US)

Date of Loss: 22 April 1952

Commemorated on Wall 2 of the Wall of Remembrance at the United Nations Memorial Cemetery – Busan, Korea

Flight Lieutenant Purssey was one of three Gloster Meteor F.8 aircraft that had undertaken a rocket attack on a large building in Chinnampo (Namp'o) when they positioned to strafe a series of motor vehicles. On striking the vehicles, two aircraft were hit by ground fire with the right wing and ventral tank of Purssey's Meteor A77-189 set ablaze.

Passing 4,000 feet his aircraft was seen to enter a steep dive followed by the right wing separating from the aircraft, sending the Meteor into a rapid, uncontrolled rolling manoeuvre. Purssey was seen to eject at 600 feet but was not seen to separate from his ejection seat before impacting the water of the Taedong River estuary. The subsequent search of the area yielded no results.

Flight Lieutenant Ian Purssey was posthumously awarded the Distinguished Flying Cross.

Pilot Officer Donald Neil Robertson

Date of Loss: 15 May 1952

Commemorated on Wall 2 of the Wall of Remembrance at the United Nations Memorial Cemetery – Busan, Korea

Pilot Officer Robertson was one of four Gloster Meteor F.8 aircraft making a rocket attack on supply lines near Masan-Ni (now called Chunghi-dong). Flying Meteor A77-373, Robertson was the second aircraft in the line astern formation as the Meteors dived on their target.

Anticipating the salvo to be fired at 1,000 feet, Robertson's Meteor was seen to prematurely fire four of its eight rockets at 3,000 feet and before the leader had commenced firing. The aircraft then veered sharply to the right at 90 degrees to the line of the attack and in a shallow dive. The aircraft broke up and exploded on impact. The following Meteor pilot witnessed the entire event and did not see the pilot eject.

Pilot Officer Robinson was posthumously awarded the United States Air Medal.

Pilot Officer John Leonard Surman

Date of Loss: 9 June 1952

Commemorated on Wall 2 of the Wall of Remembrance at the United Nations Memorial Cemetery – Busan, Korea

Four Gloster Meteor F.8 aircraft were tasked with an armed reconnaissance of a road running southeast from P'yŏngyang. Pilot Officer Surman was flying as number 4 in the formation in aircraft A77-911 when trucks were sighted on the road southeast of Hwangju.

The first pair of Meteors made two strafing passes before climbing away with the leader directing the second pair to descend and make an attack. Completing a second pass, the pilot of the preceding Meteor looked back to see Surman's guns firing and then impact the ground just short of the target. The aircraft bounced into the air before impacting the ground a second time and disintegrated in a fireball.

After circling for a period, the leader made a low pass and confirmed that the burnt-out cockpit section was 500 metres beyond the initial impact point was the only recognisable wreckage.

Pilot Officer Surman was posthumously awarded the United States Air Medal.

Sergeant Kenneth Dudley Smith AM (US)

Date of Loss: 8 July 1952

Commemorated on Wall 2 of the Wall of Remembrance at the United Nations Memorial Cemetery – Busan, Korea

Under the callsign of *Godfrey Blue*, four Gloster Meteor F.8 aircraft were tasked with an armed reconnaissance of a road following the Imjin River Valley. Smith was flying as the leader in Meteor A77-393 when he called that he had sighted trucks among the steeply rising terrain. Rolling into the attack and diving onto the target, Smith's wingman followed, albeit 2,000 feet above. The wingman witnessed Smith make his pass before pulling out with vapour streaming from his wingtips, indicating that the aircraft was being subjected to substantial G-force, possibly in an effort to outclimb the rising terrain ahead.

Smith's aircraft then impacted the ridgeline beyond the target, initially a small explosion was witnessed, followed by a large explosion as the aircraft disintegrated in flames. As the flames subsided, Smith's wingman observed a long furrow where the Meteor had traversed the ridge and no sizeable wreckage remained.

Sergeant Ken Smith was posthumously promoted to the rank of Pilot Officer.

Flight Lieutenant Frederick James Lawrenson DFC AFC

Date of Loss: 24 December 1952

Commemorated on Wall 2 of the Wall of Remembrance at the United Nations Memorial Cemetery – Busan, Korea

Flight Lieutenant Lawrenson was leading the *Redman Baker* formation on an armed reconnaissance of the Imjin River and Koksan Valley roads. Sighting a target in the valley,

Lawrenson descended his Meteor A77-852, with his wingman out to his right, to make a strafing run.

At 800 feet, the wingman sighted the tracer rounds of ground fire rising up from the right and almost immediately Lawrenson's right engine exploded with an orange flash. The wing then separated and the aircraft flick rolled and impacted a small hill where it was seen to burn for a few minutes. Lawrenson had made no radio calls immediately prior to the crash and he was not seen to eject.

Flight Lieutenant Fred Lawrenson was posthumously promoted to the rank of Squadron Leader.

Flight Sergeant John Beverley Halley

Date of Loss: 11 February 1953

Commemorated on Wall 1 of the Wall of Remembrance at the United Nations Memorial Cemetery – Busan, Korea

As one of two Gloster Meteor F.8 aircraft operating under the callsign of *Redman Able*, Flight Sergeant Halley was participating in an armed reconnaissance in the Sariwon area. Locating a number of trucks north of Sinmak, the pair made a series of strafing passes. After his final pass, Halley's wingman looked back to see a long trail of fire and what looked like a burning aircraft on the ground near the trucks that had been targeted. He called Halley but received no reply and later reported that Halley had crashed in Meteor A77-46 very close to the trucks that he had been strafing.

Flight Sergeant John Halley was posthumously promoted to the rank of Pilot Officer.

Squadron Leader Donald Hillier

Date of Loss: 8 March 1953

Commemorated on Wall 1 of the Wall of Remembrance at the United Nations Memorial Cemetery – Busan, Korea

Four Gloster Meteor F.8 aircraft were tasked with an armed reconnaissance of the Nanchooryou – Hampo-RI – Yandok area, splitting into two pairs before crossing the frontline. Flying Meteor A77-343, Hillier was the first to make a rocket pass on an armoured fighting vehicle (AFV). His wingman last saw Hillier flying straight and level at 1,000 feet but lost sight of the leading Meteor as he focused on his own attack on the AFV. He also thought he may have heard Hillier transmit 'Ah' or 'Oh' as he completed his pass.

A search ensued by 77 Squadron and other United Nations aircraft but found no trace of Squadron Leader Don Hillier or his aircraft.

Sergeant Peter Botley Chalmers

Date of Loss: 26 March 1953

Commemorated on Wall 1 of the Wall of Remembrance at the United Nations Memorial Cemetery – Busan, Korea

Sergeant Chalmers was the lead aircraft of a pair of Gloster Meteor F.8 aircraft tasked with an armed reconnaissance of the Wonsan – Singosan – Kumsong communication routes. The element descended to 8,000 feet south of Wonsan when Chalmers called that he was diving to attack a truck. As he passed over the truck, his wingman noticed that Chalmers' Meteor A77-163 was streaming white smoke or fuel which soon turned black.

Chalmers failed to respond to multiple calls from his wingman who observed the Meteor ahead flying at 200 feet. Shortly after Chalmers' Meteor dropped its left wing to a 90-degree bank angle before entering a descending turn and crashing into a small hill. The aircraft exploded on impact and burnt out in about four minutes. No parachute was observed.

Sergeant Peter Chalmers was posthumously promoted to the rank of Pilot Officer.

Flying Officer Oliver Mattison Cruickshank (Royal Air Force)

Date of Loss: 2 October 1952

Commemorated on Wall 18 of the Wall of Remembrance at the United Nations Memorial Cemetery – Busan, Korea

Flying Officer Cruickshank was flying Gloster Meteor F.8 A77-436 in a 16 aircraft formation that was tasked to conduct a rocket strike. Returning from the strike, a lone MiG-15 had jumped the formation and damaged one Meteor which subsequently returned to Kimpo.

Cruickshank reported that he was low on fuel and was heading for Cho'do to where two other Meteors had already commenced a diversion. Cho'do was an island off the coast where United States rescue helicopters were based and had served to rescue a number of US pilots who had flown damaged F-86 Sabres close to the island before ejecting.

On contacting Chodo, Cruickshank was advised to continue south to the emergency landing airstrip on Paengnyong Island, known as *Bloodstone*. However, 15 nautical miles south of Chodo, Cruickshank turned back towards Chodo and shortly after advised that both engines had flamed out and that he would be bailing out.

By this time two rescue helicopters and an amphibious aircraft were airborne. The crew of the amphibian saw Cruickshank eject at about 1,000 feet but did not sight a parachute but did witness two splashes – one was the Meteor, and the other was assessed as the ejection seat with the pilot still strapped to it. Despite being on the scene immediately, no trace of Cruickshank was found.

Flying Officer Oliver Cruickshank was posthumously Mentioned in Despatches.

Flying Officer Francis Henry Giffard Booth (Royal Air Force)

Date of Loss: 27 January 1953

Commemorated on Wall 17 of the Wall of Remembrance at the United Nations Memorial Cemetery – Busan, Korea

Flying Officer Booth was one of a pair of Gloster Meteor F.8 aircraft tasked with an armed reconnaissance of the road between Hanpori (now Kumchong) and Sariwon, while another pair patrolled a different section of the road.

Flying Gloster Meteor F.8 A77-15, Booth's leader observed two trains approaching a tunnel and initiated a rocket attack. The leader broke off the pass at 3,000 feet as he could not bring his sight to bear on the target as he encountered intense and accurate ground fire. He called out the ground fire to Booth and advised him to weave.

The leader sighted Booth making a slight weave but lost sight of him as he passed beneath at 1,500–2,000 feet. Assuming Booth was now under radar control and heading home to K14 Kimpo, the leader made another pass and was again engaged by ground fire.

Neither the element leader nor the radar controller saw or heard from Booth again following his first pass. A search failed to find any trace of Booth or his Meteor.

Flying Officer Arthur John Rosser (Royal Air Force)

Date of Loss: 28 March 1953

Commemorated on Wall 20 of the Wall of Remembrance at the United Nations Memorial Cemetery – Busan, Korea

Flying Officer Rosser was tasked with an armed reconnaissance of the road from Wonsan to Sepori. Flying Gloster Meteor F.8 A77-858 with the callsign *Peter 3,* Rosser was making a strafing pass on trucks that had been sighted on a side road. The first pass had been aborted due to turbulence and on completion of the second pass, Rosser did not report clear and did not respond to calls from the lead aircraft.

The other [pilot] climbed and began orbiting to the west of the target when a ball of grey smoke was seen rising from a small hillside. Making a pass of the site, the pilot of the other Meteor observed a black patch but could not identify any aircraft wreckage.

Flying Officer Roger Leslie James (Royal Air Force)

Date of Loss: 7 April 1953

Commemorated on Wall 19 of the Wall of Remembrance at the United Nations Memorial Cemetery – Busan, Korea

Flying Officer James was flying Gloster Meteor F.8 A77-643 in the lead flight of a twelve aircraft formation that had been tasked to conduct a rocket strike on a power station in Chinnampo (now N'ampo).

Breaking left from his rocket pass, James' Meteor was seen to emit a puff of black smoke from the left engine and then perform two slow rolls to the left. As the aircraft passed through an inverted state, pieces were observed to be falling from the Meteor. The aircraft then descended and impacted mud flats to the south of Chinnampo while inverted. Flying Officer James was not seen to eject.

Flying Officer George Peter Dollittle (Royal Air Force)

Date of Loss: 17 May 1953

Commemorated on Wall 18 of the Wall of Remembrance at the United Nations Memorial Cemetery – Busan, Korea

Flying Officer Dollittle was in a four-ship formation of Gloster Meteor F.8 aircraft that was tasked to make rocket attacks on troop concentrations northeast of Haeju. Dollittle was flying Gloster Meteor F.8 A77-856 in the attack and was seen to launch his rockets by the leader of the formation to his rear. This action was followed shortly after by a large explosion in the target area.

A large fire was subsequently observed to be burning [on] a small hill to the west and a low pass through the area identified parts of an aircraft on the ground. The pilot was not seen to eject.

HONOUR ROLL
THOSE THAT PAID THE SUPREME SACRIFICE

No 77 Squadron

Andrews, HD
Armit, ED
Avery, AJ
Browne-Gaylord, MABHA
Chalmers, PB
Colebrook, ME
Cowper, LH
Cranston, IR
Ellis, DC
Gillan, BT
Gray, WV
Halley, JB
Harrop, WP
Haslope, IC
Hillier, D
Johnston, HE
Kirkpatrick, C
Lawrenson, F
Matthews, KC
Mitchell, RD
Nolan, DT
Purssey, IGS
Robertson, DM
Robertson, DN
Robinson, RG
Robson, R
Royal, KE

Smith, KD
Spence, LT
Squiers, SS
Stephens, GI
Strange, HT
Strout, G
Surman, JL

Royal Air Force serving with No 77 Squadron

Booth, FHG
Cruickshank, OM
James, RI
Lamb, R
Rosser, AJ

No 30 Communication Unit/No 30 Transport Unit

Harding, BW
Scott, DS
Waddell, RJ

No 91 Composite Wing

McGlinchey, LT

No 491 Maintenance Squadron

Dale, H
Haines, LC

ACKNOWLEDGEMENTS

As with any major undertaking, it takes many hands to create a finished work.

In writing this book I would like to acknowledge, in the first instance, Group Captain David Fredericks who proposed the project and supported me throughout. My thanks also go to Air Commodore John Meier and his staff at the History and Heritage Branch.

I also wish to acknowledge the late Dennis Newton who had compiled a collection of many previously unpublished images from which to choose and use in this book. Dennis also created some of the original artworks.

It is important to note those authors that have preceded me in researching the RAAF involvement in what has at times been considered a forgotten war. These authors did much to highlight the outstanding effort of the RAAF in the Korean War. Among their number I would like to personally recognise Dr. Robert O'Neill (Australia in the Korean War 1950–53 Volumes One and Two), George Odgers (Across the Parallel and Remembering Korea), Col King (Luck is no Accident), David Wilson (Lion Over Korea) and Doug Hurst (The Forgotten Few). It is an honour to be associated in a small way with such esteemed authors.

The numerous veterans with whom I spoke over decades past provided immense insight, not only into operations but the day-to-day life as experienced by those that served. Col King, John Parker, Wal Rivers, Vic Oborn, Ces Sly, Keith Hill, Keith Martin, Geoff Lushey, George Hale, Peter Waugh, Bill Simmonds, Jim Flemming, and my father, Phillip Zupp, were some of those who offered these insights.

In the production of this book, Air Commodore Mark Lax and Andy Wright were invaluable in the task of editing as was Squadron Leader Steve Campbell-Wright in drawing the finished product together. This work was in turn complemented wonderfully by the artistry of Juanita Franzi.

BIBLIOGRAPHY

Bartlett, Norman (ed), *With the Australians in Korea*, Australian War Memorial, Canberra, 1954.

Blaxland, John, Michael Kelly & Liam Brewin Higgins (eds), *In from the Cold: Reflections on Australia's Korean War*, Australian National University Press, Acton, ACT, 2020.

Brown, Wayne, Andrew Cork, Colin Faggo & Annette Donselaar, *Swift to Destroy: The Illustrated History of 77 Squadron RAAF, 1941–1986*, Norman Morris Pty Ltd, Newcastle, NSW, 1986.

Cleaver, Thomas McKelvey, *MiG Alley: The U.S. Air Force in Korea*, 1950–53, Osprey Publishing, Oxford, UK, 2019.

Cull, Brian and Dennis Newton, *With the Yanks in Korea, Volume One*, Grub Street, London, 2000.

Dorr, Robert F and Warren Thompson, *Korean Air War*, Motorbooks International, St. Paul, MN, 2003.

Eather, Steve, *Odd Jobs: RAAF Operations in Japan, the Berlin Airlift, Korea, Malaya and Malta, 1946–1960*, Royal Australian Air Force Museum, Point Cook, Vic, 1996.

Evans, Ben, *Out in the Cold: Australia's Involvement in the Korean War, 1950–53*, Department of Veterans' Affairs, Canberra, 2001.

Guthrie, Ron and Col King, *Escape from North Korea: The Ron Guthrie Story*, Meteor, Australia, 2002.

Hastings, Max, *The Korean War*, Pan Books, London, 1987.

Hayes, Mike, *Angry Skies: Recollections of Australian Combat Fliers*, ABC Books, Sydney, 2003.

Hurst, Doug, *The Forgotten Few: 77 RAAF Squadron in Korea*, Allen & Unwin, Crows Nest, NSW, 2008.

Jackson, Robert, *Air War over Korea*, Purnell Book Services, London, 1973.

King, Col, *Luck is no Accident: Flying in War and Peace, 1946–1986*, Publishing Services, Loftus, NSW, 2001.

Napier, Michael, *Korean Air War: Sabres, MiGs and Meteors*, Osprey Publishing, Oxford, 2021.

Odgers, George, *Across the Parallel: The Australian 77th Squadron with the United States Air Force in the Korean War*, William Heinemann, Melbourne, 1952.

Odgers, George, *Remembering Korea: Australians in the war of 1950–53*, Lansdowne, Sydney, 2000.

Odgers, George, *Mr Double Seven: a biography of Wing Commander Dick Cresswell DFC*, Air Power Development Centre, Tuggeranong, ACT, 2008.

O'Neill, Robert, *Australia in the Korean War 1950–53 Volume One – Strategy and Diplomacy*, Australian War Memorial and Australian Government Publishing Service, Canberra, 1985.

O'Neill, Robert, *Australia in the Korean War 1950–53 Volume Two – Combat Operations*, Australian War Memorial and Australian Government Publishing Service, Canberra, 1985.

'Pilot's Notes for Mustang', RAAF Publication No. 780, Circa 1950.

'Pilot's Notes for Meteor 8 & 9', RAAF Publication, Circa 1950.

Robson, David, *Of MiGs and Men: A Brief Summary of Royal Australian Air Force Operations in the Korean War*, Aviation Theory Centre, Cheltenham, Vic, 2007.

Shacklady, Edward, *The Gloster Meteor*, Doubleday, UK, 1963.

Sutiagin, Yuri and Igor Seidov, *MiG Menace over Korea: The story of Soviet fighter ace Nikolai Sutiagin*, Pen & Sword, UK, 2009.

Wilson, David, *Lion Over Korea: 77 Fighter Squadron RAAF 1950–53*, Banner Books, Belconnen, ACT, 1994.

Wilson, Stewart, *Meteor, Sabre and Mirage in Australian Service*, Aerospace Publications, Weston Creek, ACT, 1989.

Wilson, Stewart, *Dakota, Hercules and Caribou in Australian Service*, Aerospace Publications, Weston Creek, ACT, 1990.

Zupp, Owen, *Without Precedent: Commando, Fighter Pilot and the true story of Australia's first Purple Heart*, There and Back Publishing, Bowral, NSW, 2016.

INDEX